Praise for *Faith Positive in a Negative World*

"For many people in our day, life is divided into two worlds! Their religious/ Sunday world is quite separate from the domain in which they spend the other six days of their week! In their insightful new book, *Faith Positive in a Negative World*, Dr. Joey Faucette and Mike Van Vranken show us how to bridge the gap between these realities. They offer a solid, scripture-based spirituality that can help believers to survive the challenges of the business world. "

— Most Reverend Kevin W. Vann, J.C.D., D.D.
Bishop of Orange, California

"I love this book because it clearly illustrates how to enjoy a Faith Positive lifestyle while doing business in this negative world. All Christian business leaders need to read this book to become better equipped to stay Faith Positive at all times. Using powerful illustrations, Dr. Joey Faucette and Mike Van Vranken show you how to sustain a Faith Positive lifestyle for the rest of your life as the person God designed you to be. A MUST READ!"

— Mark Whitacre, Ph.D., "*The Informant*"
COO & Chief Science Officer of Cypress Systems
Whistleblower in the historic ADM price-fixing case

"If you're ready to live a more abundant and joyful life, then read and absorb the strategies in this brilliant book! It will inspire you to reach for greatness!"

— James Mallinchak
Featured on ABCs Hit TV Show, "Secret Millionaire"
The World's #1 Big Money Speaker Trainer & Coach
Founder, www.BigMoneySpeaker.com

"This book could very possibly change your life. It is a must read for anyone who realizes that they can always improve on their skills as a businessperson, family member, or skills as a Christian. It struck a lot of nerves for me in several areas."

— Scott Foster, insurance agent, Conyers, GA

"In a world that is becoming increasingly negative, Dr. Joey Faucette and Mike Van Vranken have written a brilliant new book that will inspire and encourage all who read it. I encourage anyone needing a faith-boost to read this excellent volume."

— Dr. Robert Jeffress, Senior Pastor
First Baptist Church, Dallas, Texas

"This is one of those books that you'll dog-ear the corners, underline pages, and keep on your desk for quick reference. This is one of those books that will stir your imagination, awaken your creativity, and lead you into positive stances of work and faith. This is one of those books that comes along every so often that will impact you for ages. I am grateful for this new tool in my leadership 'toolbox!'"

— Bo Prosser, Ed.D.
Director of Organizational Relationships
Cooperative Baptist Fellowship
Atlanta, GA

I have been considered a very positive person all of my life. Others have looked to me for inspiration and encouragement. And yet, I have fallen off the positive track many times. I had to look myself in the mirror to ask "Why?" and get myself back on track. *Faith Positive in a Negative World* now is my roadmap to stay on course forever. Read this book, and then reread it over and over again, so you stay on course, too.

— TROY KORSGADEN
KORSGADEN INTERNATIONAL
VISALIA, CA

"In *Faith Positive in a Negative World,* Dr. Joey Faucette and Mike Van Vranken show you very clearly how to realign your thoughts, beliefs and life with the positivity that wraps up our spirituality and gives it an unmistakable radiance. This positivity is our faith. You will benefit greatly from discovering the powerful tactics uncovered in this transformational read. Dive in and watch your world change for the better right before your eyes!"

— BETH MISNER, BEST-SELLING AUTHOR & BNI FOUNDATION CO-DIRECTOR
JESUS AND THE SECRET

"It is so easy to lose hope in our world today. Van Vranken and Faucette in *Faith Positive in a Negative World* give us a clear, direct and scripturally-based wisdom on how to stay hopeful. Their teachings on how to look for the good and to find opportunity in whatever situation we find ourselves in is a wisdom that will serve Christian business professionals well their whole lives."

— MOST REVEREND MICHAEL DUCA, BISHOP OF SHREVEPORT, LA

"Set your mind on things above by reading *Faith Positive in a Negative World.* You can achieve great things for the Kingdom and your business by taking captive your thoughts and making them obedient to Christ. This book will help you get your thinking in the right direction."

— JULIE BELL, PHD, AUTHOR, SPEAKER, COACH
RENEWED, GIVING GOD YOUR BEST BY TRAINING THE MIND OF A CHAMPION PERFORMANCE INTELLIGENCE AT WORK
THEMINDOFACHAMPION.COM

"If you're finally ready to build your dream business, then make sure you read *Faith Positive in a Negative World* by my great friend, Dr. Joey Faucette, and Mike Van Vranken. When you implement the five core practices of a Faith Positive lifestyle you'll quickly discover that you have a lot more help than you ever imagined in building your God-sized business."

— JIM PALMER, YOUR DREAM BUSINESS COACH
WWW.DREAMBIZCOACHING.COM
PHILADELPHIA, PA

"I found this book useful in combining the principals in the Bible with practical ways to do business."

— AL CLARK, INSURANCE AGENT, ARLINGTON, TX

"Success is about controlling the things you can control, so you can cope with the things you can't. *Faith Positive in a Negative World* is a practical and inspiring guide to enable you to accomplish your work and enjoy your life to His glory!"

— BARBARA HEMPHILL
FOUNDER, PRODUCTIVE ENVIRONMENT INSTITUTE

"*Faith Positive in a Negative World* is a MUST READ if you wish to grow your faith, build your business or advance your career. Based upon proven Biblical principles, its loaded with positive energy to counteract the negative world we live in."

— MICHAEL PODOLINSKY CSP, CSPGLOBAL
ASIA'S PRODUCTIVITY GURU
WWW.MICHAELPODOLINSKY.COM
SINGAPORE

"I've always heard that one good idea makes a book worth it. Well, that means that *Faith Positive in a Negative World* is worth a fortune! In a few pages I picked up multiple ideas that will revolutionize the way I think about my work. I enthusiastically recommend this book!"

— ROCKY GILL, FRANCHISEE/FRANCHISE DEVELOPER
EXPRESS EMPLOYMENT PROFESSIONALS
TYLER, TX

"Are you a Christian in the business world? Do you want to deepen your faith? Are you ready and willing to leaven the negativity of the marketplace? Read FAITH POSITIVE IN A NEGATIVE WORLD, the new collaboration of Joey Faucette and Mike Van Vranken. Their five core practices will guide you clearly and powerfully toward your spiritual dreams."

— DR. BOB DALE, EXECUTIVE COACH, RICHMOND, VA

"All too often the world of faith and the world of work seem planets apart. In a practical down to earth way, *Faith Positive in a Negative World* enlightens our minds and inspires our hearts to better connect our Sunday worship with our Monday work."

— TOM NELSON, AUTHOR OF *WORK MATTERS*
LEAWOOD, KANSAS

"Finally, a practical guide for business owners that uses spiritual concepts! *Faith Positive in a Negative World* shows you how to integrate your faith with work for a more balanced you! This book is intriguing and an easy read that has deep, lasting meaning. Thank you, Dr. Joey and Mike, for helping me to reconnect the "light" in my business and personal life."

— DEBORAH MILLER, INSURANCE AGENT
LAKE HAVASU CITY, ARIZONA

"In *Faith Positive in a Negative World*, Dr. Joey Faucette and Mike Van Vranken have creatively focused on the 4 pillars that adversely impact the Christian life personally and professionally: worry, fear, faithlessness and impatience. They provide a positive approach for transforming the pillars into a fulfilling life and career that God intends when we stand firm and allow Him to direct our pathway. This book is a *must* read for everyone searching for positive answers and guidance in their personal and business lives."

— HERMAN DIXON, RETIRED INSURANCE EXECUTIVE, COACH AND AUTHOR
PRINCIPLES OF LIFE AND LEADERSHIP MY CAT TAUGHT ME
HTTPS://THINKBIG-COACHING-TRAINING.COACHESCONSOLE.COM
CHARLESTON, SC

"Back in my editor days, Joey Faucette was one of my best writers. Joey continues his long history of quality writing with *Faith Positive In a Negative World*. In this excellent new book, Joey and Mike Van Vranken tackle the subjects of work, faith and attitude in engaging, relevant, practical, and helpful ways."

— MARTIN THIELEN, UMC MINISTER AND AUTHOR OF *WHAT'S THE LEAST I CAN BELIEVE AND STILL BE A CHRISTIAN?* AND *THE ANSWER TO BAD RELIGION IS NOT NO RELIGION*
COOKEVILLE, TN

"Dr. Joey and Mike have a unique ability to hold up a very humbling and sometimes humorous mirror that I often need when work and life squeezes in. Their sincere approach to applying God's principles remind me to be thankful when I lose sight of the tremendous blessings He has provided in my life. "

— KEITH FOLMAR, INSURANCE SALES LEADER, STATE COLLEGE, PA

"I'm like you. I spend the majority of my waking hours at work. How do I follow Christ in the workplace when the rest of the world seems to be going the other direction? The truth is Christ called us to be salt and light everywhere and not just on Sundays. Dr. Joey Faucette and Mike Van Vranken in *Faith Positive in a Negative World* go beyond "why" and give us "how" to be salt and light at work. This book hits a home run for those of us wanting to live the full life Christ calls us to live."

— DAVE ANDERSON
ANDERSON LEADERSHIP SOLUTIONS
TYLER, TEXAS

"Dr. Joey Faucette has done it again with this book! He hits the nail on the head time and time again to bring focus to the power of being positive, no matter what chaos and negativity might be going on around us. This time he's teamed up with Mike Van Vranken, esteemed mentor and coach, to give us ways to keep the faith in the workplace for greater joy, deal positively with negative people and our own self-destructive thoughts, and allow us to receive all that God intends for us. The secret is in serving others, which is something I agree with fully. I can recommend this book to Christians in the business world and anyone who needs to shift their mindset to the positive so they can reach their success goals in and out of the workplace. Excellent and uplifting read!"

— J. MASSEY, INVESTORPRENEUR, AUTHOR, SPEAKER, MENTOR, COACH, EDUCATOR
WWW.CASHFLOWDIARY.COM

"Successful leaders develop the critical discipline of thinking through significant challenges with a positive perspective. In the practical pages of *Faith Positive in a Negative World*, Dr. Joey Faucette and Mike Van Vranken bring the positive perspective of God's Truth to fuel leadership thinking that transforms."

— MELVIN ADAMS, PRESIDENT, RENEWANATION, ROANOKE, VA

"What a joy to read *Faith Positive in a Negative World*. It inspires me to read about businesspersons who look at everything in a positive manner instead of in a negative world. I was excited to read it and even more excited to know how I could apply the practices to my life and business."

— KATRINA ROBINSON, INSURANCE AGENT, SHREVEPORT, LA

"A famous philosopher (Mark Twain) once said 'Few things are harder to put up with than the annoyance of a good example.' *Faith Positive in a Negative World* is a real annoyance, especially if you are miserable and hate your job or work. It asks you to risk it all in faith with joy in your work and love for the One that gave it to you. To focus through the fog to receive abundance and say "no" to negativity. And what's worse? The authors live and breathe this *Faith Positive* stuff. Read the book. Be prepared to be annoyed."

— STEVE KAYSER
AUTHOR AND FOUNDER OF KAYSER MEDIA
CINCINNATI, OH

"Dr. Joey and Mike provide the tools you'll need to build a successful business and happy life. My application of them has bestowed countless blessings upon my business, clients, and family. As you follow them, you will do the right things for the right reasons, and achieve success and spiritual fulfillment in all endeavors."

— MARY STEWART, MBA, PRESIDENT
MARY STEWART HEALTHCARE CONSULTING, INC
INDIANAPOLIS, IN

"*Faith Positive in a Negative World* reminds business leaders that we must maintain a servant's heart to be shared with our organizations and ultimately the customers we serve."

— DREW DAVIS, INSURANCE AGENT, LEESBURG, FLORIDA

"Need a place to start? This book is chock-full of "do-ables" - bite sized actions, habits and changes to help you live as a positive person of faith in what is too often a negative world of work. Digest it for yourself; share it with your fellow pilgrims."

— PEGGY HAYMES, AUTHOR
"STRUGGLERS, STRAGGLERS AND SEEKERS" AND
"I DON'T REMEMBER SIGNING UP FOR THIS CLASS"
GREENSBORO, NC

"*Faith Positive in A Negative World* provides exactly what the believer needs to "recalibrate" in the midst of all the negative forces we face each day. The summaries at the end of each chapter plus coaching boxes with questions to ponder provide opportunities to dig deeper and explore issues that may be causing the world's pull to take its toll on you. After all, you can only address what you identify! I recommend this read for anyone who is looking for encouragement along their journey of faith and for those who recognize that negativity has crept into your once vibrant work life."

— CHRISTINE KENNEDY, LEADERSHIP & LIFE PURPOSE COACH, LYNCHBURG, VA

"Dr. Joey Faucette has done it again! Following his #1 Amazon best-seller, Dr. Joey has teamed with Mike Van Vranken to write an outstanding, biblically-focused book that helps Christian business professionals work in faith. Their "how to" core-values for achieving joy in the workplace are based on permission-giving Scriptures that are central to our faith and ethics. Positive change is possible in the workplace with *Faith Positive in a Negative World*. I look forward to sharing it with Christian business people everywhere!"

— THE REV. BRUCE TUTTLE, PASTOR AND FORMER DIRECTOR OF CONGREGATIONAL
DEVELOPMENT, VIRGINIA CONFERENCE, THE UNITED METHODIST CHURCH

"Would you like to know how to have a lifestyle where your 'work and faith can partner together in a positive way?' Dr. Joey and Mike Van Vranken have captured the practical solutions to give you a daily "blueprint" for living and working "in" this negative world without being "of" it! Take advantage of this important book that will increase your faith and change the way you face and handle your work, so you can have greater joy to love God and others more!"

— SUE FALCONE, OWNER
"SIMPLY" SUE SPEAKS! GLOBAL BOOKING AGENCY
GREENSBORO, NC

"Early in the Preface sits a powerful paradigm waiting for you to embrace: *You perceive mentally new solutions to old business challenges by focusing on the positive and filtering out the negative.* You have choice. It is one of God's gifts to you. How you use it is your gift back to Him. Make it an awesome one. That is what Dr. Joey Faucette and Mike Van Vranken have done with this dynamic book."

— BOB NICOLL, WORDSMITH, AUTHOR
CREATOR OF REMEMBER THE ICE
LAS VEGAS, NV

"This book is a wonderful reminder that, as a small business owner, my Christianity does not stop at the door of my business. The authors gently prompt us to proudly lead our employees and clients with a servant's heart. I love the examples demonstrating that the foundation of our success must be based on this core practice."

— ANNETTE HAYES, INSURANCE AGENT, OPELOUSAS, LA

"Today's business environment is filled with confrontation and dilemma. I do not believe this is the way we should work and live. What if we used our faith in our everyday activities, in business and in pleasure? Would our accomplishments be many instead of few? Would our pressures become pleasures? Would business flourish? I believe that *Faith Positive in a Negative World* opens the door to what is possible through faith in business, but more importantly in life."

— MARTY LAMBERT, PREMIER NETWORK, CHARLOTTE, NC

"Not only do Dr. Joey and Mike Van Vranken perceive the *problems* we face at work... they also perceive--and graciously share--the *solutions.* Through prayer, praise, and maintaining a positive outlook, we can achieve our dreams and faithfully fulfill our calling even in a toxic environment."

— JORY H. FISHER, JD, PCC
WWW.JORYFISHER.COM
BALTIMORE, MD

"Dr. Joey Faucette and Mike Van Vranken have scored the most important point of all, reminding all of us that a some-time faith is really a no-time faith. Full-time faith has to include our work life. This is a sure guide for marching off of the map of an ordinary workplace and into a new world of caring and serving, creating a new work-community."

— MACK MCCARTER, FOUNDER/COORDINATOR
COMMUNITY RENEWAL INTERNATIONAL
SHREVEPORT, LA

"Living out your Christian faith in the workplace is challenging. *Faith Positive in a Negative World* gives you practical strategies on integrating your faith into the workplace and transforming your entire business."

— JOHN WILLIAMS, PASTOR
RIVERVIEW CHURCH, PHOENIX, AZ

"The world of business will greatly benefit from the God-sent messages in this book."

— RON NEWSON, INSURANCE AGENT, SLIDELL, LOUISIANA

faith positive in a negative world

redefine your reality and achieve your spiritual dreams

Joey Faucette and
Mike Van Vranken

Listen to Life
Publishing

Listen to Life Publishing
Editor: Judi S. Hayes
Cover Design: Will Oakes and Andrew Welyczko
Production and Design: Rebecca Fitzgerald
Author Photos: Alice Abbott Photography (Joey Faucette) and Harrington House Photographic Studio and Gallery (Mike Van Vranken)

This publication is designed to provide accurate and authoritative information with regard to the subject matter covered. It is sold with the understanding that the publisher is not engaged in rendering legal, accounting, or other professional services. If legal advice or other expert assistance is required, the services of a competent professional person should be sought.

Unless otherwise indicated, all Scripture quotations are taken from THE MESSAGE. Copyright © by Eugene H. Peterson 1993, 1994, 1995, 1996, 2000, 2001, 2002. Used by permission of Tyndale House Publishers, Inc.

Scripture taken from the New King James Version®. Copyright © 1982 by Thomas Nelson, Inc. Used by permission. All rights reserved.

Scripture taken from the HOLY BIBLE, NEW INTERNATIONAL VERSION®. NIV®. Copyright © 1973, 1978, 1984 by International Bible Society. Used by permission of Zondervan. All rights reserved worldwide.

Scriptures marked KJV are from the King James Version of the Bible.

Givers Gain® is a registered trademark, and has been reproduced with permission, of BNI Enterprises, Inc.

Library of Congress Cataloging-in-Publication Data
Faucette, Joey and Van Vranken, Mike
     Faith Positive in a Negative World: Redefine Your Reality and Achieve Your Spiritual Dreams/by Joey Faucette and Mike Van Vranken
         p.   cm.
         ISBN-10: 0971507449
         ISBN-13: 978-0-9715074-4-9
         Spirituality 2. Business. I. Title.
         Library of Congress Control Number 2014913191

Printed in the United States of America

Mike

To God, Barbara and Emily – all three;
whose love and devotion have fostered my
Faith Positive life.

Joey

To my parents, Becky and Lonnie Faucette,
for telling me the stories of Jesus,
and showing me how to live them.

Joey

Contents

Contents

SECTION 2

CONCEIVE THE POSITIVE IN FAITH AT WORK

SECTION 3

BELIEVE THE POSITIVE IN FAITH AT WORK

SECTION 4

ACHIEVE THE POSITIVE IN FAITH AT WORK

SECTION 5

RECEIVE THE POSITIVE IN FAITH AT WORK

FOREWORD
Bishop Kevin W. Vann
Orange, California

Living our Faith in our daily lives has its moments of challenge, yet also moments of "wonder and awe" (to use one of the gifts of the Holy Spirit, for example).

In St. Matthew 's Gospel, Chapter 6:25 and following, we have the well-known words of The Lord to remind us of the uselessness of worry. This is certainly in contrast to the necessity of seeing The Lord's presence in all situations and trusting that "all will be well" as Julian of Norwich said centuries ago.

Mike Van Vranken, a graduate of the University of Dallas in Irving, Texas (where I was a member of the Board of Trustees) and Dr. Joey Faucette invite us to do just that in this book, which is a reflection on Faith and daily life.

For many people in our day, life is divided into two worlds! Their religious/Sunday world is quite separate from the domain in which they spend the other six days of their week! In this insightful new book, Dr. Joey Faucette and Mike Van Vranken show us how to bridge the gap between these realities. They offer a solid, scripture-based spirituality that can help believers to survive the challenges of the business world.

With an approach that abounds with practical examples and solid scriptural references, these authors show us that our prayer life and our professional life don't have to be disengaged from one another. Each chapter begins with a scriptural focus and ends with reflective questions, as they help us to perceive, conceive, believe, achieve, and receive the positive impact of faith in our work environment!

Most Reverend Kevin W. Vann, J.C.D., D.D.
Bishop of Orange, California

You Can Be Faith Positive

How is it we all do business in the same world and yet do it so differently?

Some of us are "of the world"—no opportunities, nothing will work out right, negative?

While others of us are "in the world"—overflowing opportunities, everything will work out fine, positive?

What makes the difference?

Linda started her own business, which became successful financially, but at a great cost. She rarely took a complete weekend off and never took a vacation. Her husband and two young children went on trips without her.

After five years she decided that now was the time to take a vacation and enjoy some extended time off, getting to know her husband again and enjoying her children. So she called her three vice presidents in for a meeting and told them, "As you know, we've all worked hard to grow this company. I've ensured through these five years of hard work that each of you had some time away. But I didn't do for myself what I did for you.

"So the time has come for me to take an extended vacation. I'm taking the next year off to enjoy my family. The only way I can reasonably do this is to leave each of you in charge of running your departments.

"While I'm gone, I expect each of you to carry on as if I were here. And as an added bonus, I've deposited money in your department's account. Jill, you'll find $50,000 to invest in the business as you see fit. John, you're receiving $20,000 to invest in the business as you deem appropriate. And Bob, you'll find $10,000 to invest using your talents to grow this business. I'll be back a year from now and expect an accounting at that time." And Linda got up from her desk and left.

Jill, John, and Bob sat dumbfounded for a moment and then stumbled over to the window overlooking the parking lot. "There she goes," Jill said. "She's really doing this."

"And for a whole year," John said. "Who would have thought it?"

Bob said, "Must be a trick or a test of some sort. She'd never leave us alone for that long with that much additional money."

Jill turned away from the window. "Well, you guys can stand here if you want to, but I've got $50,000 to invest in this business so I'm going to get busy." She walked out the door, down the hall, and toward her office.

"Yeah, me, too," said John, as he pulled out his smartphone to make a call, walking down the hall to his office.

"I still think it's a trick or something," Bob said, as he stood there in Linda's office.

A year passed more quickly than Linda imagined it would. She found herself back in her office, meeting with Jill, John, and Bob again. After chatting about some of her vacation highlights, Linda said, "OK, Jill, tell me what you did with my $50,000 while I was gone."

Jill pulled up a spreadsheet on her tablet, threw it on the screen, and said, "Linda, I invested it in marketing a new division within our company to an underserved target group. You'll see at the bottom of this sheet that I doubled your $50,000. There's $100,000 profit there."

"Great work, Jill! That's exactly what I had hoped for. And because of your marvelous achievement, Jill, I'm making you a partner in the company. Here's a contract for you to read over and let me know what you think. Now John, it's your turn. What did you do with my $20,000 while I was on the beach relaxing?"

"You're gonna love this, Linda," John said as he pulled up a spreadsheet on his phone and also threw it on the screen. "When you left, I studied our inventory liquidity and discovered we've got some items that hang around a little too long in our warehouses, clogging up our cash flow. So I invested in new software and hardware for an updated inventory control system, negotiated with our vendors for tighter shipping, and well . . . you can see for yourself."

"Wow, John! You turned that department around $40,000 by solving that problem. You are awesome, John. So let me do something awesome for you," and she handed him a contract. "Read this over and let me know what you think about becoming a partner in the company. Bob, it's your turn. Tell me something good!"

"Well, Linda," Bob said hesitantly, "I know you have high standards, and I know you hate carelessness. You demand the best and don't tolerate a lot of mistakes. I was afraid I would disappoint you, so I wrote a check for the $10,000 you left me and put it in the company safe. And here it is, safe and sound—your $10,000."

Linda's face turned red, then scarlet. "Bob," she said slowly, "I've been gone a whole year, and the best thing you could do with $10,000 is to let it sit in the company safe?"

"Yes," Bob said. "It's all there."

"The least you could have done," Linda said while standing up, "was to have put it in a money market account somewhere. But you couldn't even do the least, could you, Bob? At least I would have gotten a little interest."

"I just thought it best to play it safe," Bob said.

"Play it safe?" Linda asked. Then she took a deep breath

and said, "You know, Bob, you're right. Play it safe. Great policy. I'm going to play it safe, too."

She handed the $10,000 check to Jill and said, "Jill, here's $10,000. Invest it as you think best."

Then turning to Bob she said, "Bob, I'm going to play it safe some more. Go clean out your desk. You won't go out on a limb for me so I can't go out on one for you. Take your things and leave. I can't afford to have you around any longer."

Same situation. Same circumstances.

What makes the difference?

When Jesus originally told this story, he has "Linda" saying to "Bob":

"It's criminal to live cautiously like that! . . . Take the [ten thousand] and give it to the one who risked the most. And get rid of this 'play-it-safe'" (Matt. 25:26, 28). "For to everyone who has, more will be given, and he will have abundance" (25:29, NKJV).

What makes the difference?

Risk. To risk it all in faith with joy in your work and love for the One who gave it to you.

To be "in the world but not of the world" is to risk everything to increase your faith with greater joy at work so you love God and others more. You risk that God can be trusted, that your relationship with Jesus Christ is credible, and that the Holy Spirit really can help you discover the wisest path.

You risk it all to achieve your spiritual dreams . . . even at work.

This risk may seem large to you. Perhaps too large. Work is in a category of its own, separate from the spiritual which belongs at church or in a small group. You have to take care of work by yourself. Increasing your faith at work to improve your bottom line or paycheck like the businesspersons in Jesus' story isn't relevant in this negative world today. Greater joy at work is a pipe dream for you. You belong to the two-thirds of U.S. workers who say they're very dissatisfied with no sign of improvement. And as for loving God and others more, "Well, Dr. Joey and Mike, sure I love God, but you guys don't work where I work. Loving the people I work with and our customers is impossible."

We understand it's a risk. A bigger risk for some than others.

Here's what we know from years of coaching: Christian business professionals often depend on the negative world to determine their success just as non-Christians do. They abdicate their God-given birthright to achieve fulfillment through work to the naysayers of negativity who chronically find something wrong. They let "of the world" blueprint their "in the world."

Do you want to increase your faith with greater joy at work so you love God and others more but just don't know how?

Kinda hard to do with 24–7 business news channels reporting economic Armageddon daily. Local TV news at 6:00 AM and PM importing doom and gloom. Your newspaper's lead headline making you sick to your stomach. Talk radio and its Chicken Littles reporting "the sky is falling" so don't get out of bed. You can drown daily in a news tsunami whose mantra is, "If it bleeds, it leads."

You didn't have to turn on the TV or radio or pick up a newspaper. You know the world is negative. Even Jesus said so: "For what profit is it to [you] if [you] [gain] the whole world . . . ?" (Matt. 16:26, NKJV).

The world is negative.

And you're trying to do business in it and be Christian.

How's that working for you?

Yea, we thought so.

That's why this book is so important for you right now.

Sure, there are a ton of problems to tackle that are of this negative world. We live east of Eden. However, if we continue to bring the same work models to them, we get more of what we already have.

It is time for a better way to be in the world but not of it.

That's the big promise of this book: your work and your faith can partner together and make a more positive life for you, your family, and the world.

You can enjoy a Faith Positive lifestyle.

The purpose of this book is to coach you as a Christian business professional to tap your faith and create a positive way of working in this negative world. To create a movement of people just like you who get out of the negative world and in faith work positively. People who overflow with joy at work so others want to do business with them. People like you who manifest Christian love for others because you realize how much God loves you in Jesus.

You join the movement of Christian business professionals bringing faith, joy, and love to the negative world. You practice the five core practices of a Faith Positive lifestyle:

1. You mentally perceive new business solutions to old challenges by focusing on the positive and filtering out the negative.

2. You relationally conceive business with other positive people and discover ways of delivering these new solutions.

3. You emotionally believe your business reality can be redefined and your spiritual dreams fulfilled in a vibrant faith reality.

4. You physically achieve your spiritual dreams, strategically acting at work.

5. You realize that you receive so much faith, joy, and love, you say, "Thank you!" and give positivity by serving others, offering a new work ethic to the world.

And amazingly, the Faith Positive cycle turns again, and you find yourself receiving even more.

That's how you are in the negative world and not of it, increasing faith with greater joy at work so you love God and others more.

To positively transform yourself and the world, you strategically implement these five core practices of a

Faith Positive lifestyle at work. The institutions you once depended on to supply you with faith, joy, and love are less relevant in today's world.

It is our turn as Christian business professionals to claim our place in the negative world as positive, bright lights set on a hill. To continue the movement begun by ancient folks who worked—fishermen, tax collectors, tent makers, merchants, farmers, lawyers—and took the good news message of working with Jesus to the negative world. Christian women and men who before the professionalization of clergy claimed it as their privilege and responsibility to share faith, joy, and love at work, who understood that working as a Christian is the greatest sermon ever preached.

Are you willing to take the risk? This risk that makes all the difference between those who succeed in the world like Jill and John and those like Bob who are of the world and don't succeed?

Jesus said it's criminal to work like play-it-safe Bob. And, "to everyone [like Jill and John] who has, more will be given, and [they] will have abundance" (Matt. 25:39, NKJV).

You can have this abundant life in the negative world starting now. The great truths written in this book are eternal. Meditate on them. Discover reading pit stops along the way to do just that. Ponder your Faith Positive work for a moment. Idle in the pits for a few minutes or a few hours. Consider how well you're increasing faith with greater joy at work so you love God and others more while you refuel.

As you refuel, share what you're pondering. On Twitter, use #FaithPos to mark your comments. Join the LinkedIn group, "Faith Positive Professionals." Or "like" and post on the Facebook fan page, "Faith Positive."

Find the "Grab and Go" summary at the end of each chapter. These quick statements give you a mile marker to return to when you want a quick, refreshing drink of positive energy.

Join others reading this book and in the Faith Positive

Master Coaching Program and discuss your discoveries in Christian study groups through work or your church community.

Enjoy a Faith Positive lifestyle while doing business in this negative world. Take the risk and positively succeed starting now.

perceive the positive in faith at work

Perceive the Positive in Faith at Work

"And the peace of God, which surpasses all understanding,
will guard your ... minds through Christ Jesus."

—Philippians 4:7, NKJV

Your Faith Positive lifestyle begins in your mind. You perceive the positive in faith with your thoughts.

Dr. Joey's family enjoys setting up a backyard bird feeder in the winter. The problem is that squirrels love bird feeders or, more specifically, birdseed.

So Dr. Joey waged war on the birdseed-stealing squirrels one winter. He started looking out the bay window for the mangy tree rats so he could grab an air rifle, sneak outside around the corner of their home, and shoot them. He even put his four-year-old daughter on alert: "Honey, let me know if you see a squirrel on our bird feeder."

Until one day she said, "Daddy, we used to look out the window for pretty birds. Now we look for ugly squirrels."

When she said that, Dr. Joey realized that all the joy of

the bird feeder was gone. He wasn't looking for pretty birds and their magnificent colors anymore but ugly squirrels.

It's easy to see only the ugly squirrels that invade work to steal the seed of your joy. They will steal your positive faith at work if you let them.

It's easy to stop looking for the beautiful opportunities to increase your faith in God, to cease listening for the joyful songs—the cha-ching of the cash register or the relieved tone in a customer's voice when you solve a problem, to miss the brilliant colors of the loving relationships you enjoy with customers and teammates alike.

You decide what will fill your mind—the beautiful or the ugly.

Your Faith Positive lifestyle of working in the world, but not of the world, begins in your mind with the thoughts you perceive, the first core practice.

Ponder Your Faith Positive Work for a Moment   #FaithPos

Remember a work experience when you looked for the ugly instead of the beautiful. What can you learn about how you work in the world but not of the world?

CHAPTER 1

Focus Your Thoughts

*"Let petitions and praises shape your worries into prayers,
letting God know your concerns."*
—Philippians 4:6

You've played the game where someone mentions an object—a dancing bear wearing a pink tutu—and tells you not to think about it. Of course, what's the first thing that flashes in your mind? That dreaded dancing bear wearing a pink tutu. Your mind focuses your thoughts quickly with little suggestion.

So, why is it such a challenge to perceive the positive in faith and focus your thoughts on greater joy at work?

Unless you discipline your mind—that is, train it to focus on the positive—it will hone in on whatever attention grabber presents itself. That's why Paul says, "Instead of worrying, pray." Your mind focuses in one of two ways: you worry (negative) or you pray (positive).

Here's how your mind works. You watch a report on a business channel that says the economic sky is falling. The company you work for has grown stronger for the last six consecutive quarters.

But what do you do when your vendor calls to confirm your next quarter's order? You worry and shrink the order despite the business's success.

Or let's bring it home. You're watching TV, and a commercial comes on for your favorite snack food. The next thing you know, you're heading to the kitchen for that snack food.

Your mind received the impression, activated a hunger impulse, and triggered your legs to move. You really didn't even think about it. It just happened.

But what if you positively focus your thoughts, the spiritual equivalent of prayer? Let's say you made the decision to cut out snacks between meals because your metabolism has slowed significantly at middle age. Your mind is made up before the commercial airs. You think about getting a snack but decide against it because it is more important to be healthy than to chase a snack commercial into the kitchen.

Perhaps you're thinking, It's not that easy to focus my thoughts, especially when it comes to faith and work.

Actually it is. Your mind was made to focus and does so every minute, even when you're sleeping. The key is to choose how you focus: positive prayer or negative worry.

Want to increase your faith with greater joy at work so you love God and others more?

Focus on the positive and pray.

Focus knowing that you see what you choose to see.

Ever test-drive a new car and suddenly see that make, model, and color everywhere?

Buy a new dress or tie, go out, and there it is?

Decide on a name for your unborn child and suddenly every newborn in your area has that name?

Think of prayer as a way to focus your thoughts so you see the positive. Paul writes, "Let petitions and praises shape your worries into prayers, letting God know your concerns. Before you know it, a sense of God's wholeness, everything coming together for good, will come and settle you down. It's wonderful what happens when Christ displaces worry at the center of your life" (Phil. 4:6–7).

You see what you choose to see as you pray. You focus your thoughts on increasing your faith. How?

By talking with God about petitions and praises. Petitions are easy to focus on. Those work situations that worry you flood your mind as you close your eyes and bow your head. The tsunami of petitions overwhelms your prayers.

Turning the tide to praise requires a choice. A mental effort. A conscious shift in spiritual intention that blows in a different direction.

Oh yea, you think. Let me praise you, God, for that contract yesterday.

The negative storm subsides. The sun peeks out between the dark clouds of despair. And your mind focuses on a positive experience to praise.

Petitions and praises prayed. You settle down from the negative into the positive. Christ displaces worry at the center of your work and life.

You focus on the positive, knowing you see what you choose to see.

Your faith increases. You have greater joy at work. You love God and others more.

And yet maybe you're thinking: Come on guys. It's not that easy. You don't work where I work. My faith is challenged every day. Joy left a long time ago. And who has time to love God and others?

Yes, it's difficult to have a Faith Positive lifestyle in this negative world. Someone or some situation always wants to steal your joy at work.

Dr. Joey enjoyed some quiet time early one morning before the demands of the day started. All of a sudden a bird began making all kinds of noises just outside the window. At first he ignored it. Finally he got up to investigate.

As he stepped out on the porch, he saw the bird—a baby mockingbird—perched in a Japanese maple, squawking at Maybelle, the family cat, who sat on the porch, staring off across a horse pasture. The bird that bothered Dr. Joey didn't bother Maybelle at all.

Maybelle saw Dr. Joey on the porch and sauntered over, rubbing herself against his legs, asking, "Pet me!" which he did while she purred. The baby bird still screamed, but Maybelle just didn't mind. She focused on the beauty of that quiet morning, the petting and purring rather than the noisy bird. She knew the bird was there but chose to ignore it.

Someone at work is always squawking, challenging you to focus on a Faith Positive lifestyle. You go to work, and a squawking team member is complaining about the cheap coffee. Or a squawking manager thinks you're a superperson who can leap tall workloads in a single bound. Or a squawking customer is convinced you overcharged her a nickel.

Focusing your thoughts on the positive is challenging at such times, especially when you are the one doing the squawking.

From early in his career, Mike desired to be in a leadership position with the company. He reached an executive position and looked at his next target: to become a vice president.

While he prayed unceasingly, the opportunity never came. He forgot to focus on the joy of his current work as he focused on the vice-president position. He forgot to praise God for what was one of the best jobs in the country. His focus was blurred by his own squawking.

Eventually the opportunity to become a VP came and went. As it did, God showed Mike that despite his internal squawking, something better was coming. He would have had to move his family to another part of the country had he been promoted. He would have missed being close to his parents before their deaths. Being away from his only daughter would have been difficult.

Another calling for Mike emerged as the squawking subsided and he settled down in peace. Mike earned his master's degree in theological studies and prepared himself for writing this book and his current ministry work.

Mike praised God with thanksgiving because he was not promoted and still does daily. As God promised, peace filled his heart despite the squawking.

Petitions and praises. Settle down. Christ displaces worry.

Even when you are the one doing the squawking, you can focus on the positive in faith. Yes, negative things still happen. That's business east of Eden. You choose to let them suck the joy out of work or focus on the thoughts of blessings.

The choice is yours. The jet fuel that powers your mental focus, imagination, is equally good at focusing on the positive and the negative at work. It really doesn't care which it focuses on. It simply follows the trail you guide it down.

More is required than simply removing your negative thoughts. To increase your faith with greater joy at work, you quickly discover that your imagination abhors a vacuum and works to fill it. Usually it fills your mind with worry.

Just remove the negative thoughts without positive, replacement thoughts and you get worry. Worrying about your work focuses you on negative potential outcomes that may or may not become reality. Your mind requires filling with something. You can choose to focus on the positive.

Petitions and praises. Settle down. Christ displaces worry.

Prayer focuses you on the positive, increasing your faith with greater joy at work so you love God and others more.

Ponder Your Faith Positive Work for a Moment #FaithPos

What were you worried about at work last year about this time?

Focus through the Fog

You can pray and choose to focus on the positive, ignoring the squawking negativity at work to boost your joy. But what happens when your imagination demands more information and sometimes you don't have it? You allow your thoughts to follow the rabbit of your imagination down into a dark hole.

If you're the owner: "What if the bank calls my note due early because I had a down quarter?"

If you're the manager: "What if my key employee quits to start his own business?"

If you're a team member: "What if my spouse says I'm never home and leaves me because I have to do three people's work now?"

What happens when you descend into this imaginary hole of negative worry? A mental fog seems to roll in, and because you cannot see into the future far enough to satisfy the insatiable appetite of your imagination, worry slips in on cat's paws.

Or horse's hooves.

The kitchen in Dr. Joey's home overlooks a hill across a horse pasture. It's really beautiful … except when the fog rolls in. Then you can't see down the hill and across the pasture, which means you can't see the horses and make sure they're safe. That's when his and his wife's imaginations start asking for more information than is available, and worry rolls in with the fog:

A snake could bite a horse on the nose.

A horse could step in a hole and hurt itself.

One could get sick and die because the vet wasn't called in time.

The list goes on and on.

Of course, none of these things have ever happened, with or without the fog. But because the fog blocks their vision, they worry.

Are you that way at work?

You worry about the "What if …?" future of your work. And yet so far in your career, few if any of these things have actually happened.

That doesn't keep you from worrying, does it? You allow your imagination to morph into worry and take control of your mind, and negative thoughts crop up.

It happens to all of us.

That's why Paul writes to his Philippian friends to choose petitions and praises rather than worries and frets. But how do you do that?

Mow Your Negative Broomstraw and Sow Positive Seeds

Petitions and praises. Settle down. Christ displaces worry.

Dr. Joey got on his tractor on a beautiful winter day and mowed a portion of a horse pasture. Now you may be thinking, Guys, nothing grows in a pasture over the winter.

Actually, broomstraw can. The soil nutrients get a little off from what's best for growing grass, and broomstraw emerges in the winter. It competes with the spring grass for nutrients, water, and sunlight. Horses eat grass and pick around the broomstraw. So you mow the broomstraw in winter to eliminate the competition for growing spring grass.

When your imagination morphs into worry and takes control of your thoughts, negative thinking crops up like broomstraw. It competes for the nutrients in your mind.

Have you ever noticed that one negative thought breeds another? And another? And pretty soon, an entire field of negative mental broomstraw is growing in your mind?

Think of prayer as mowing your negative mental broomstraw and sowing positive thought seeds. The positive thoughts of Christ grow taller and crowd out the negative worry.

You can choose to mow down your negative thoughts and plant positive thoughts. We call it the "mow and sow" way to pray. With just ten minutes in the morning and ten minutes in the evening, you increase your faith with greater joy at work so you love God and others more. You work in the negative world, but you're not of it.

Start your morning by finding a quiet place to focus your mind on positive thoughts for ten minutes. First, you mow. Avoid all "push media" such as TV and radio in the mornings. Remember, their mantra is, "If it bleeds, it leads."

Mow your negative mental thoughts by leaving the TV remote and radio alone.

Then sow positive thoughts by taking the first five of your ten minutes to read something positive or listen to positive music. Think of this as your positive mental breakfast. It jump-starts your mental metabolism with positive thought nutrition. Opening work e-mail or surfing through all of your friends' rants on Facebook doesn't qualify. Your faith increases or decreases, your joy at work is lesser or greater, and your love for God and others ebbs and flows based on your choices.

Of course, the Bible is a fantastic source of positive reading. We read Scripture every morning and even have phone apps that serve up our bookmarked favorites. Other books are valuable, also.

Listening to some favorite tunes also sows positivity into your day. Ever have a song stick in your mind? If it's a positive one, it encourages you to be Faith Positive all day.

Set up a playlist of your favorites on YouTube as we have. That way you just pull it up on your smartphone and play it again.

In your first five minutes of ten in the morning, you mow by avoiding radio and TV and sow by reading positive literature or listening to positive music. With your second five minutes, pray with your schedule for the day in mind. Mow your negative worries for the day by sowing positive outcomes into each appointment. Hear yourself at the end of the day saying, "Well done!" as you increased your faith. Visualize positive results from each conversation with greater joy at work. Feel a sense of spiritual satisfaction, more love in your heart for God and others.

Petitions and praises. Settle down. Christ displaces worry.

Next, set aside ten minutes in the evening before you go to bed to think positively about your day's experiences. Each evening get in bed ten minutes before you want to go to sleep. Or, if you're like us, sit in a chair so you avoid going to sleep. Relax and name three things you're thankful for that happened that day. Plant in your mind an attitude of gratitude that cultivates in your sleep overnight for these three blessings.

This mental exercise has the marvelous effect of mowing and sowing simultaneously. Sowing three positive experiences from the day crowds out any negative, worrisome broomstraw. To ensure you crowd it out, avoid watching the evening news or a "bloody" TV show before bedtime. Keep it light. Detox your brain from the day.

Be as specific as possible when recalling your three positive experiences. Instead of saying, "I'm thankful for my wife," say, "I'm thankful for my wife and her generous gift of time in running three errands for me today." Or let's say you're an insurance agent. Instead of just saying, "I'm grateful for all my new friends who bought policies today," say, "I'm grateful for my friend Louise, who signed a policy today for herself, one on each of her children, and promised to send her best friend to do the same."

Being specific helps. You will feel more refreshed than usual the next morning because you put these positive thoughts of gratitude into your mind and processed them overnight.

Writing down these three positive experiences helps plant them more deeply in your mind. Dr. Joey prefers pen and paper while Mike puts it all in his tablet. Whether you type or write, name it "The Gratitude Diary" and keep it as your record of positive stories. Write enough to be able to come back in a year or more when you're scratching your head, wondering if you ever had any positive experiences, and read and remember. The mental benefit of reminding yourself is huge on those evenings when there are more petitions than praises. That's why we call it "The Gratitude Diary."

One of Mike's favorite Gratitude Diary entries is a trip to Europe he enjoyed with his daughter. They attended a play in one of the most crowded sections of London one Saturday evening. As they left the theater around 11:00 PM, she suggested they walk the four or five miles back to the hotel.

Mike realized in about an hour that they were lost in a dangerous part of the city. There were no cars on the streets. The only other people they saw were exiting underground establishments because the street-level buildings were all boarded up. That's when he got scared.

So there they stood on a dark sidewalk, searching in every direction for the way back, with no idea how to find their hotel.

In a soft voice, Mike said, "Angels, I need you here, and I need you now."

Suddenly, a black London taxicab came down the street out of nowhere. The driver stopped, insisted they get in the car, and offered to take them to their hotel.

They got in and the cabbie asked, "Do you like my new cab? It only has seven miles on it." It's almost midnight and this guy has a brand-new car with only seven miles on it!

Next he asked, "Have you seen any Aston Martins since you've been in town?" Aston Martins have been Mike's favorite car since he was twelve years old. You can see every car imaginable in London. How did he know to ask about this particular car? It was as if he knew them.

They made it to the hotel, and before Mike could pay him, the cabbie explained it was a custom in London that whenever a driver gets a new cab, the first fare is free. They thanked him and prayed God's blessings on him. He winked at them and drove off.

It was almost 1:00 AM by this time, and Mike and his daughter were safely back in their hotel. He asked her, "Do you realize we just had an angel rescue us?" They talked about it and agreed God sent an angel to protect them.

Fifteen minutes later, Mike's daughter sat up in bed and said, "Now you're not going downstairs in the morning and tell everyone an angel brought us home, are you?"

Of course he did, which is part of why this one is a favorite Gratitude Diary entry for Mike. You'll have some exceptional experiences like Mike's to write about, and you will spend some evenings scratching your head and wondering, "Did anything positive happen today?" Sure, it did. It might be something like, "I didn't get run over by a concrete truck today," or "My key still fit the lock on my home's backdoor." Keep focusing your thoughts back through the day because you may have, like Mike and his daughter, "entertained angels unawares" (Heb. 13:2, KJV).

Ponder Your Faith Positive Work for a Moment   #FaithPos

What do you currently do that feeds your mind positive perceptions daily?

Will you try these two suggestions: start each day by opening your mind, and end each day with gratitude? When will you begin?

Focus on the Good Soil

As you mow the negative mental broomstraw and sow positive thoughts for ten minutes each morning and evening, sometimes you will experience more success than others. Some days it's easier to read Scripture and pray over your schedule. Other mornings you can hardly pull back the covers. Some evenings you can hardly write your three positive experiences quickly enough. Other evenings you are just glad to have the day done.

These Faith Positive, perceive core practice strategies work. It's just that sometimes they fall on a tough day.

It was autumn, the season for Dr. Joey to plant grass seed in the horse pastures. He bought some sacks of good seed, loaded them in the spreader on the tractor, and scattered it everywhere he could.

He noticed in the days following that the horses had beat down a path through the pasture. They walk that same path every day so it's a hardened path where no grass grows. Since the ground was hard, the birds came and ate the grass seed off the path.

Some of the seed he scattered wound up in a pile of rocks collected from the pasture and stacked up around the base of an oak tree. It grew pretty quickly but only into tiny sprouts. The roots were shallow, and the hot spring sun scorched the sprouts.

Some of the scattered seed went outside the fence line and over into a thick area where blackberry thornbushes grew. The grass took root and shot up for a little while but just couldn't compete for sunlight and nutrients with the taller, more mature blackberry bushes. It died.

The rest of the seed fell on parts of the pasture that were good soil. They grew in the spring, took solid root, and kept growing. It wasn't too long before the horses could go back into that pasture, and they just loved all the new grass.

After reading this chapter, you may have one of several reactions:

"I just don't get it, all this talk about how my mind constantly focuses on something all the time." You have been "of the negative world" so long you are like the path the horses beat down—hard—so the good seed of this chapter can't penetrate your worry-dominated mind.

You might say, "Yeah, I love it!" and start focusing your thoughts for ten minutes in the mornings and evenings so you can enjoy a Faith Positive lifestyle, achieve a little success, and say, "I got it," and put this book down. Your experience will be like the grass that grew in the rock pile. When the heat of adversity from the negative world overwhelms you—and it will—you wilt.

You may say, "I'm going to turn my thoughts away from the negative," but not choose to fill your mind with positive thoughts. Worry rolls into your imagination like fog. The weeds of worry choke your imagination and keep you from positively growing your faith, joy at work, and love for God and others.

Or perhaps you read this chapter and say to yourself: "This is really good stuff. I'm focusing my thoughts on positively increasing my faith, joy at work, and love in relationships, but I want more." You, my friend, are ready for a beautiful growing experience that will feed you an increasing faith with greater joy at work so you love God and others more—far more than you can imagine.

Keep reading.

Ponder Your Faith Positive Work for a Moment   #FaithPos

Be surgically honest with yourself and answer these questions:

Which of the four responses listed above am I experiencing right now at work?

Which of the four responses listed above do I want to have?

Which one will allow me to increase my faith with greater joy at work so I love God and others more?

Grab and Go

As you focus your thoughts, remember:

1. Your mind focuses with just a little suggestion. Seen a dancing bear wearing a pink tutu lately?

2. You see what you are looking for in your work.

3. Prayer focuses your thoughts on the positive at work.

4. Worry fogs your perception about your work.

5. Mow the mental broomstraw out of your mind about work. Then sow good seed with your ten minutes in the morning (positive reading and prayer) and in the evening (The Gratitude Diary).

CHAPTER 2

Avoid Only Familiar Thoughts

"No one cuts up a fine silk scarf to patch old work clothes."
—Luke 5:36

D o you remember when your third-grade teacher showed you all those multiplication tables and said you had to memorize them? What was your reaction? "No way," right?

Today you know them. You carved out some new neural pathways in your brain. You created a new folder named "Times Tables."

How did you do it?

Superefficient or Basically Lazy?

You can see your mind as superefficient or basically lazy. Either way, here's what happens mentally as you perceive your faith at work:

1. A perception of how you do faith at work enters your mind.
2. Your brain begins to sort the information.
3. The sorting process includes searching through previously stored information. Your mind wants

to place this new information in a folder labeled "Familiar."

4. If it does not fit in a current category and your brain has no idea where to file it, it tries to throw it out or at least put it in the "Recycle Bin" in hopes that you empty and delete it later.

5. At this moment you say, "I don't understand," or "I've never done it this way before." You label the unfamiliar as "Negative," and toss it.

The unfamiliar of the changing world intrudes daily into your work. How do you deal with it and increase faith with greater joy at work so you love God and others more?

Ponder Your Faith Positive Work for a Moment   #FaithPos

What has changed at work for you in the last year?

Repeat after Me

You deal with the changing world at work the same way you learned your multiplication tables: repetition.

You sat down and thought those tables over and over until you got most of them correct.

"Now was that so hard?" the teacher asked.

"Yes," you said. Even as a third-grader, you knew how difficult it is to create something new in a brain that longs for the familiar.

It requires a great deal of effort to hack your neural way through the jungle of the familiar to plant something unfamiliar. Your brain begs for the familiar and really tries to exclude anything uncharted. Your mind doesn't want you to march off the map of previous experiences because that's where danger lurks, where the wild things of work are.

So here you are, reading a book titled *Faith Positive in a Negative World*, hoping to figure out a way to successfully increase your faith with greater joy at work so you love God and others more. Your thoughts may be negative, thinking, *That's of the world.* Negativity is familiar. Yes, it's miserable, but you choose the familiar regardless.

You want to grow your faith with greater joy at work, perhaps because it's more difficult to love God and others or what once worked no longer does. You desire positive faith results and crave greater joy at work. You're praying that there is more to doing business than what you're experiencing. You realize to do faith in a different way, you can't keep doing the same old behaviors, and yet your mind doesn't care whether you are negative or positive about your faith at work. It only longs for the familiar. So how do you overcome its love of the negative world's familiar?

Repetition.

You repeatedly choose to think positive about your faith at work and focus your mind on those aspects that, though they may be unfamiliar, are success stories. Just as you did with your multiplication tables, you create some novel neural pathways that over time become familiar.

Ponder Your Faith Positive Work for a Moment   #FaithPos

Recall a recent experience in which you learned something new whether it was how to operate a new piece of equipment, run some new software, or beat your son at the new Madden Football game.

How often did you say, "I don't know how to do this!" or "I've never done this before?"

Easier Said Than Done

Mike struggled through four back surgeries over three years before he could sit, walk, and even sleep for more than an hour or so. The six-inch surgical scar on his back was an ugly area of his body he hid from everyone. He was convinced the hideous mark would nauseate anyone. Every time he saw it, he slid down the dark hole of familiar, negative thinking.

Then he heard a minister talking one day with someone who had a terrible, embarrassing scar on her arm. She could hardly go out in public because of it. "What if," the minister suggested, "you see your scar as a rainbow from God? A reminder of the healing you received, left by God as a reminder of his great love for you?"

Mike's thinking about his own scar transformed immediately. The unfamiliar—the scar as a sign of God's love—suddenly was worth repeating.

Before his surgeries Mike had been told he may never walk again and have to apply for disability. Now his scar reminded him of God's miracle of healing. Daily he thought of his scar in an entirely new way. Sure, it took a few weeks of repeating to himself how beautiful his scar is, and yet he eventually smiled every morning as he saw the stunning rainbow God gave him as a permanent image of just how much he is loved.

New challenges come daily as you try to increase your faith with greater joy at work so you love God and others more. At first you judge them negatively simply because they are unfamiliar like Mike's scar. They fail to fit your preconceived notions of how to do faith, be joyful at work, or show love.

You resist the change, only to wake up the next morning and discover that yesterday's change has been joined by today's, and tomorrow's change lurks in the shadows, ready to pop out when the clock strikes midnight.

The mantra "I've never done it this way before" is absolutely true. Redefining this reality from one of resistance to change to one of "That's right, and if I want to increase my faith with greater joy at work, I'd better learn how to do it this way" is absolutely critical if you're going to do business, much less enjoy a Faith Positive lifestyle, in and not of the negative world today.

Ponder Your Faith Positive Work for a Moment   #FaithPos

Consider how you have reacted to something different at work or maybe something personally embarrassing like Mike's scar. How could God transform your reaction to something more Faith Positive?

What Is Your Typical Reaction to Something Unfamiliar?

Your mind perceives the familiar first and longs for it, even if it is negative.

You avoid thinking familiar, negative thoughts only through coaching your mind to search out the positive aspects of doing faith with greater joy at work and repeating them until your brain stubbornly creates a new file folder.

Here's how it works. Mike's Lebanese grandmother taught him how to make the family's favorite Middle Eastern dishes when he was about nine years old. He memorized with care every ingredient and the proper way to combine them to create the perfect dish. And, while he loved every single kind of Lebanese food imaginable, they all included onions.

Onions make Mike sick.

He always included onions whenever preparing those handed-down recipes for his own family even though he got sick. After all, that's the way his grandmother taught him to do it.

Mike decided around his fortieth birthday that doing it the way he had always done it really wasn't working well. So, as difficult as it was not to follow his grandmother's recipe, he created his own Lebanese masterpieces without onions. He now enjoyed the dishes more without getting sick.

Thinking only familiar thoughts kept him from the joy of eating without onions. He was imprisoned by comfortable habits, even though they had negative outcomes. He freed himself from his grandmother's ways and found an entirely new and better way of celebrating his heritage.

Why had he waited so long? It seems like a no-brainer today. Then it was unfamiliar.

Sometimes your faith-at-work life is only familiar, and that's led to negative thinking that's of this world. Until one day, in a moment of spiritual discovery, you find that you can stir some new ingredients into your habits and just enough unfamiliar positivity to deliciously deliver a delightful dish to those with whom you're working.

When you make this discovery, when you perceive an unfamiliar, positive thought and your negative illness dissipates, repeat it.

Over again.

And again.

Avoid only familiar thoughts. After all, your reasoning of "just because I've always done my faith that way at work" must not be working, or you would be reading something besides this book.

Perceive unfamiliar thoughts that may seem awkward at first but result in more faith, joy, and love at work.

Then celebrate because you've just taken another step in your journey toward your Faith Positive lifestyle, discovering how you can increase faith with greater joy at work to love God and others more, while doing business in a negative world.

Embracing the Unfamiliar

When you read the Gospels, particularly Luke, you discover that the Pharisees and religious scholars favored the familiar. They kept things kosher. They defended the status quo.

So when Jesus invited Levi, a hated tax collector, to "come, follow me" and the moral reprobate dropped his coin purse and walked with Jesus, you could have bought the Status Quo Border Patrol for a nickel. To make matters worse, Levi threw a sumptuous dinner party with the finest china, crystal wine goblets, and gold-plated utensils stolen tax money could buy. And then he had the audacity to invite every tax-collecting friend and other "despicable me's" he knew … plus Jesus! This Jesus, who increased faith so radically with an unfamiliar joy in his work that showed more love for God and others, could perhaps help save his friends from themselves, too.

The champions of correctness couldn't stand idly by while this defiant assault of their familiar by the unfamiliar occurred. From Levi's front yard, they said loud enough to one another to be overheard by those in the big house, "What is he [Jesus] doing eating and drinking with crooks and 'sinners'?" (Luke 5:30).

Do you hear the lust for the familiar way of perceiving faith, joy, and love at work? "Religious workers don't act like this," they said.

Jesus stuck his head out the door and said, "Who needs a doctor: the healthy or the sick? I'm here inviting outsiders… to a changed life, changed inside and out" (Luke 5:31–32).

Can you imagine how quiet things got around the dinner table about then? Surely Levi smiled. He got it. Faith, joy, and love at work are unfamiliar and yet necessary to redefine the reality of the negative world.

Surely his reprobate friends got it, too. Jesus was talking about them. They knew they were sick and needed a doctor. But not just any doctor. One whose faith, joy, and love for his work were accessible to them.

Realizing they were losing, a scholar said, "John's disciples are well-known for keeping fasts and saying prayers. Also the Pharisees. But you seem to spend most of your time at parties. Why?" (Luke 5:33).

"No one cuts up a fine silk scarf to patch old work clothes," Jesus said. "You want fabrics that match" (Luke 5:36).

Change is unfamiliar. It's frightening to your mind because you prefer the old work clothes of the way you've always done it. Change gives you a headache because you have to repeatedly perceive the unfamiliar, intentionally choosing to suspend your judgment in pursuit of the positive. Through repetition you force your brain to form new categories and file the positive until it becomes familiar.

You know it's the only way to increase your faith with greater joy at work so you love God and others more. What you've been doing no longer positively works ... by a financial or spiritual bottom line. You want the fine silk scarf, the new fabric that matches.

You want to be Faith Positive in this negative world, not of it.

You can start today to avoid only familiar thoughts. Just give yourself some time to embrace the unfamiliar.

Dr. Joey's wife received some new horses to board. The previous farm was set up differently with the four horses in a much smaller area, daily walking a space that measured about one hundred feet by one hundred feet. So when she put these horses into a five-acre pasture, you would think the first thing they would do would be to run all over it, happy to be in a larger space.

Not so fast. At first the lead horse in the herd stood in one spot all day. In his mind he was still in a small space so he didn't move.

When he did move a few days later, he walked a one hundred foot by one hundred-foot perimeter—the same size space he occupied previously. He was still a prisoner in his mind of the small space. Even though he was unhappy, he could not yet escape his familiar patterns.

After a couple of weeks, he began to explore the larger pasture. Step-by-step, he expanded his space to include part of the unfamiliar pasture. Through repetition he became more and more comfortable. Gradually his mental picture expanded.

After about twenty-one days he burst into a gallop through the pasture with reckless abandon, kicking up his heels, toward the fence line at the far end of the five acres. When he arrived at the fence, he stood there for a moment, admiring the view. Then he turned to look back at where he had been, nickered to the other three horses, and they galloped to him.

You want to be Faith Positive. Your heart's desire is to increase your faith with greater joy at work so you love God and others more.

Please remember that your brain is superefficient and lazy.

Your mind perceives the familiar first—the way you've always done faith, joy, and love—and longs for it like old work clothes and the old pasture, even if they were negative.

You avoid thinking familiar, negative thoughts only by throwing repetitive parties in your mind, inviting the unfamiliar, positive thoughts to pull up to your table. You need a doctor, one who brings an inside-out change of a new faith, joy, and love that's accessible to you and as fine as a silk scarf.

If Levi and a herd of horses can accept the positive unfamiliar, so can you.

Just remember that while Levi went immediately, you might need twenty-one days like the horses.

And that's okay.

Ponder Your Faith Positive Work for a Moment   #FaithPos

Relive a recent experience in which you faced a change at work and after a while successfully navigated in faith through it. Put yourself back into the struggle of the change, but also revel in the joy as you positively emerged on the other side. Recall your customers' faces as you provided a new solution to their problems. Relive the team's looks as the change actually worked. Recall the joy you experienced as you showed love to others. What was that experience like?

Grab and *Go*

As you avoid only familiar thoughts, create a new mental file folder for these unfamiliar thoughts:

1. Change is unfamiliar. Of course, you've never done it this way before.

2. Welcome unfamiliar thoughts with repetition.
    Welcome unfamiliar thoughts with repetition.
    Welcome unfamiliar thoughts with repetition.

3. Focus on your scars or rainbows. Your choice.

4. Levi's house for dinner? Or dining with Pharisees and scribes?

5. How big is your work pasture?

CHAPTER 3

Filter Your Thoughts

"Do [your] best by filling your minds and mediating on …
the best, not the worst; the beautiful, not the ugly;
things to praise, not things to curse."

—Philippians 4:8

There was Dr. Joey, chainsaw and weed trimmer in hand, hacking away at undergrowth attacking the fence line around a horse pasture. He noticed a sapling growing up under it. He reached for the chainsaw and, just before cranking it, looked back at the sapling and studied its leaves. It was a maple sapling, the kind of tree that blazes orange in the fall.

Dr. Joey grew up in a part of the world where pine trees grow like weeds. Pine trees look the same all year long. Hardwoods like maples are rare in that area. Even after all these years of being gone, maples in the fall are a novelty to him.

He put the chainsaw down and picked up a shovel to dig up the maple sapling and transplant it to another place on the farm to enjoy its beauty. He aimed the shovel at the sapling, and noticed something growing beside it—poison ivy.

Have you ever touched poison ivy? It causes a miserable itch that lasts for weeks.

So Dr. Joey stood there, thinking about what to do next, when he realized that there they were: irritating poison ivy and a beautiful maple tree growing in the same soil, side by side. Something beautiful growing right beside something ugly. The best in nature nurtured next to the worst. Something that prompts praise nestled alongside something to curse.

Just doesn't seem right, does it?

And yet the soil did not care what's planted in it—a maple tree or poison ivy. The soil nourishes and grows whatever it receives.

Your Mind Is like Soil

You can choose to plant poison ivy—only familiar, negative thoughts that erupt in itches of worry and cause the worst in faith scratching, an ugly loss of joy, and a cursing of love loss. Or you can choose to plant maple trees—unfamiliar, positive thoughts that increase your faith to its best, with beautiful joy at work and love praises for God and others. Your mind nourishes and grows whatever it receives.

Your first step to a Faith Positive lifestyle is choosing to perceive the positive in faith—in, but not of, the negative world. Your mind focuses your thoughts every second, and you now know the importance of aiming that focus on the positive as you pray. Your mind craves the familiar, even if it is negative, and you now understand how to carve out new neural, positive pathways because you, like Levi and the horses, want all of the faith, joy, and love that's accessible.

After you focus your thoughts and avoid only familiar thoughts in faith at work, you next filter your thoughts. When you focus your thoughts through prayer, you turn away from the negative and toward the positive. When you avoid only familiar thoughts, you search out unfamiliar thoughts and in faith welcome them. The reality of doing business today is that sometimes you turn away from a negative thought and run right into another one. You keep turning, only to discover that you are surrounded by negativity. And sometimes as you avoid only familiar thoughts, you bump into so many familiar, negative thoughts that you wonder how you will find your way out and into the Land of Unfamiliar.

What do you do then?

You filter your thoughts.

Ponder Your Faith Positive Work for a Moment   #FaithPos

Identify a recent experience in which you were in a negative conversation at work and joined in by adding to the already downward spiraling talk. What were you thinking and feeling as you walked away?

What You Resist Persists

There is a saying, "What you resist, persists." That is, when you focus your thoughts on not being negative, you concentrate on the negative. For example, when you tell yourself, "Now don't forget to … ," your mind zeroes in on the word "forget." And what do you usually do? Forget it.

When you tell yourself, "Now remember to … ," your mind takes aim at the word "remember." And what do you usually do? Remember it. It's more than a denial of the negative. It's a filtering of the negative in order to affirm the positive. By resisting, you focus on the negative. By filtering it, you acknowledge it and choose the more positive.

Remember the dancing bear in the pink tutu we suggested you not think about? And how it popped into your mind immediately?

Bob Nicoll tells the story of walking into a convenience store one hot summer day in Phoenix and seeing a sign above the cash register, "Don't Forget the Ice." He asked the manager how his ice sales were. "Slow," the manager said, despite the fact that it was about 110 degrees in the shade.

So Bob asked for a piece of paper and a marker. He created another sign that read, "Remember the Ice." He asked the manager to remove the current sign, put up the new one, and see if that helped sales.

When Bob returned to the store in about three weeks, the manager was so excited to see him. "I've tripled my sales of bags of ice," he said, "and it's all due to your great sign! Thank you!" (Discover more at www.RemembertheIce.com.)

What you resist, persists. Poison ivy grows at work. It's inevitable east of Eden. You have customers, teammates, maybe even a boss who irritates you. These poison ivy relationships grow in the same soil as your maple tree relationships. You filter out the poison ivy by refusing to plant it and, when it does grow, by uprooting or spraying it with herbicide and choosing instead to plant and nurture the maple trees.

Filtering your thoughts to keep out the negative and let the positive pass through increases your faith with greater joy at work so you love God and others more. Negativity is in the world. It's Pollyanna at best and stupid at worst to think otherwise. What you resist, persists.

Baseball pitching great Warren Spahn was battling the New York Yankees in the 1958 World Series. The Yankees' Elston Howard came up to bat. Spahn's manager came out to the mound and said, "Whatever you do, don't pitch it high and outside."

The great pitcher tried to rethink the instructions to "pitch it low and inside," but it was too late. The thought "high and outside" dominated his mind. His next pitch— you guessed it—was high and outside. Howard hit a single and, later that inning, scored the winning run.

How important is it to filter your thoughts? The next day the Yankees won the World Series.

To focus on the positive and filter out the negative is a choice you affirm daily, sometimes hourly. Resisting the negative is futile. You focus on it more. Filtering the negative to focus on the positive increases your faith, joy, and love with continual praying.

Think about filtering your thoughts this way. Tons of

sand and dirt were being moved at the beach while Dr. Joey and his family were on vacation. A company was replenishing the beachfront with sand from the ocean floor because of a hurricane's erosion. Pumping in tons of dirt from the ocean floor made the shallow shore water murky and dirty looking.

Dr. Joey and his younger daughter went down to check out the ocean. It was so muddy you couldn't see your feet or anything else even in the shallow water. It was so muddy he said to his kindergarten-aged daughter, "Yuck! Look how dirty the ocean is."

She said, "But Daddy, it looks like a chocolate ocean to me."

He looked down at the water again and this time saw it differently. The water really did look chocolate brown. He and his daughter looked at the same ocean but with two entirely different perspectives.

He saw, "Yuck!"

She saw, "Yum!"

She filtered out the obvious and thought beyond it to discover the positive.

You have a choice about how you perceive the positive in faith at work—yuck or yum. Your mind will grow either you choose. You filter according to what you choose to enjoy in your Faith Positive lifestyle.

Ponder Your Faith Positive Work for a Moment   #FaithPos

What are you resisting right now at work? Be surgically honest as you think about it.

One way to filter out the negative and focus on the positive is to change your perspective. As you do, the filter of your thoughts unclogs. Dr. Joey learned the value of a new perspective as he painted the board fencing around a horse pasture one day. He bought a five-gallon bucket of stain and lugged it up and down the fence line as he smeared it with a four-inch brush.

He painted one side of the fence and then went to the other side. There wasn't a gate close by in one section, and he really didn't want to carry the heavy bucket up the hill to the gate.

So Dr. Joey decided to lift the bucket up over the fence, putting it down on the other side, and then climbing over the fence. He got the heavy bucket over the top board of the fence, but as he stretched farther and farther to let it down, it tipped and spilled stain on the ground.

He climbed over the fence, looked at the mess, and from his new perspective on the other side of the fence, noticed that the bottom of the fence was high enough for him to have slid the bucket under the fence.

He thought, *I wish I had a second chance to do that over.*
Do you ever wish for a do-over?

Sure you do. You do something at work and get results you didn't want. You gain a new perspective and realize what you could have done. Then you want a do-over to unclog your perception filter.

A Great Thing about Your Faith Positive Lifestyle

One of the great things about increasing faith with greater joy at work is that you discover do-overs. The mistakes you make deciphering the success code of loving God and others more are an expected part of your learning curve. You learn something from a new perspective that helps you unstop your filter. Then you find yourself in a similar situation and you do it over, this time with the benefit of what you learned previously. Yes, you make mistakes. You just make new ones.

What do you think Dr. Joey did the next time he was far from a gate? He checked out which was better, lift the bucket over the fence or slide it under.

You filter your thoughts, reflect on previous experiences

and what you can learn from them, and that determines what you allow to pass through your filter—the positive— and what you filter out—the negative.

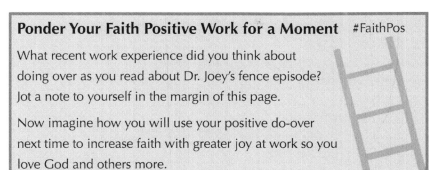

Ponder Your Faith Positive Work for a Moment   #FaithPos

What recent work experience did you think about doing over as you read about Dr. Joey's fence episode? Jot a note to yourself in the margin of this page.

Now imagine how you will use your positive do-over next time to increase faith with greater joy at work so you love God and others more.

Neglect your filter and your faith decreases with diminishing joy and less love.

Think about it this way. Let's say before you start your vehicle each morning, you put six grains of sand in your gas tank. OK, it's only six grains of sand, but if you do it every morning, how long do you think it'll take before your vehicle won't run? Soon, right? That great engine would be a mess, incapable of taking you anywhere.

Negative thoughts of the world dropped into your mind affect you in the same way. They break down your mental motor with worry. Pretty soon you can't go anywhere.

As you filter your thoughts, you prevent even tiny grains of negativity from entering your mental engine. You selectively leave them out, not resisting them, but proactively choosing to avoid allowing them to come inside and play with your faith.

When you filter out the negative perceptions, you choose a positive path to success. Or you can invite the negative inside your mind unfiltered and watch your faith sink, your joy shrink, and your love stink.

It's your choice.

That's why Paul advises us to "do [your] best by filling your minds and mediating on ... the best, not the worst;

the beautiful, not the ugly; things to praise, not things to curse" (Phil. 4:8).

Your mind will grow whatever you plant in it.

Your work will grow whatever you plant in it.

Your growth at work reflects your mind's growth.

Choose to filter your thoughts and plant the positive and watch your faith increase with greater joy so you love God and others in ways you can only imagine now.

Grab and Go

As you filter your thoughts, weave your filter with these thoughts:

1. Plant maple trees in your mind, uproot the poison ivy, and watch your work colorfully grow.

2. "What you resist, persists."

3. Perceive the "yum" (chocolate ocean), not the "yuck" (murky water) at work.

4. Take advantage of the do-overs and plant what you learn into your next work experience.

5. Focus on the positive and filter out the negative.

conceive the positive in faith at work

Conceive the Positive in Faith at Work

"We take our lead from Christ...He keeps us in step with each other."
—Ephesians 4:15

In the last section you discovered the perceive core practice of your Faith Positive lifestyle. Your mind naturally focuses on the familiar, and yet you can choose to focus it on the unfamiliar and filter your thoughts to fill your mind with the positive. You can focus on the positive and filter out the negative. You can fill your mind with, as Paul described it, "the best, not the worst; the beautiful, not the ugly; things to praise, not things to curse" (Phil. 4:8).

As you fill up your mental tank with high-octane, positive thoughts, you find yourself with others in the negative world who experience opportunities to make identical mental choices. Some choose positive thoughts. Some don't.

And you have been with them all along.

Do you remember your mother and father getting up at two o'clock in the morning to feed you? Those experiences when you were an infant lying in a crib, screaming your head off because your stomach is growling, and suddenly this

39

bleary-eyed person appeared over your crib, reached down, picked you up, and held you close. You felt the warmth of that embrace. You heard a soft voice. You were fed. The next thing you knew, you fell asleep again, back in your crib, totally satisfied and happy. Do you remember that experience?

Of course not. Even though it happened night after night for months, depriving your parents of much-needed sleep, these gracious acts of compassionate kindness your parents offered just because they loved you slip through your memory.

Despite your lack of remembering them, they still happened along with other acts of cooperation. A diaper changed. A sippy cup of juice poured. Long hours worked to buy you new jeans or pay your car insurance.

All of these completely cooperative acts combine to make you who you are today—a wonderful, unique human being capable of a Faith Positive lifestyle.

However alone you may feel at times in your faith journey at work, someone is with you. You were created to be in cooperative relationships. You didn't arrive at your current life's mile marker as a solo driver. You have traveled in a carpool the whole time.

As you focus on the positive and filter out the negative mentally, your carpool includes relationships with positive-focused and negative-focused people. Who do you attract more? And how do you deal with the negative people so you increase your faith with greater joy at work?

The second core practice of developing your Faith Positive lifestyle is about how you conceive positive relationships at work.

Ponder Your Faith Positive Work for a Moment #FaithPos

When was the last time you became anxious about getting something done? So anxious you tried to accomplish the task alone, without the benefit of the people around you, some of whom knew what to do? How did that work out?

CHAPTER 4

Cooperate Completely

"And He Himself gave some gifts to be apostles, some prophets, some evangelists, and some pastors and teachers, for the equipping of the saints for the work of ministry."

—Ephesians 4:11–12, NKJV

You were created to enjoy a Faith Positive lifestyle through relationships with others.

Your success at work depends on your attracting customers, teammates, and suppliers with whom you conceive a Faith Positive business. Your next step, now that you're focusing on the positive and filtering out the negative as you embrace unfamiliar thoughts, is to discover how to conceive the positive by cooperating completely with others.

This cooperation challenges familiar notions of achieving positive success as a self-made person and pulling yourself up by your own bootstraps. Despite its familiarity, this notion is a myth.

Ponder Your Faith Positive Work for a Moment #FaithPos

Remember a time of struggle or challenge in your work, a time your thoughts were more negative, like, "I'm all alone in this," or, "No one can help me with this business problem." Who appeared to help? How did this person assist you?

Something You Miss

Cooperating completely with others presupposes that you know partially, that you are incomplete alone and complete with others. That your puzzle piece at work contributes to the picture, fits nicely into other pieces, and requires them to complete the picture. If you passionately want to achieve your spiritual dreams, you redefine your egotistical reality of "I already know that" to "Please show me how."

One day a blue block of frozen material crashed from the sky into a farmer's field. He cut off a chunk of it, put it in his freezer, and called the sheriff. He was convinced it was something extraterrestrial, but all he really knew was it stunk when it melted.

The sheriff examined it and didn't have a clue, so he called a chemistry professor from the local college. The professor took a sample from it to analyze and call back with the results. The farmer kept the blue frozen material in his freezer. He just knew he had discovered the key to life in an alien universe.

The chemistry professor called the farmer. "Sir," she said, "your blue frozen material is definitely not extraterrestrial so you can relax. And please take it out of your freezer and throw it away as soon as possible."

"Why?" the farmer asked.

"Because, sir," she said, "what you have in your freezer is the portable toilet fluid ejected from a plane as it flew over your farm."

One of the most essential ingredients of our cooperative

conceiving of the Faith Positive lifestyle is that no matter how much you positively perceive, and think you perceive accurately, you miss something, just like the chemistry professor and the farmer.

Paul talked about our creation for cooperation when he wrote that Jesus gave different abilities or roles to various people to serve on Faith Positive teams, citing examples like prophets and teachers, apostles and evangelists. You need others to achieve your spiritual dreams in the negative world. When you're "of the world," you waste time and energy pulling on your own bootstraps.

So how do you discover your God-sent team members who want to increase faith with greater joy at work so together you love God and others more?

Ponder Your Faith Positive Work for a Moment   #FaithPos

Recall an experience in your work life when you received what you required with little effort. What was that like for you?

Whom Do You Attract?

Conceiving your Faith Positive lifestyle consists of more than just your efforts alone that generate positivity. You are in relationships already that validate, confirm, and even expand your positive perception. You literally were born into these relationships, created to cooperate completely both with the God-created universe and those in it. Living into these positive relationships is the key to conceiving your Faith Positive life.

The key to leveraging these relationships is to focus and filter your thoughts in such a way that you become the kind of person you want to attract onto your team. You become the person that is like the persons you want to do business with as customers or clients, employees or employers, and vendors or suppliers.

Use these questions to shape yourself to conceive your increasing faith with greater joy at work with positive partners:

1. What are my core values? That is, those character traits you want to exhibit in your business relationships? What would your family members say are your core values?

Think of your core values as the spiritual drivers for how you do what you do at work. Such qualities as honesty, integrity, faith, joy, and love motivate you.

Paul sees these as the stimulus for using your gifts at work. They prompt you to equip others you attract for service using their gifts. Others serve from their gifts, which are different from yours. The shared core values unify you in the midst of these diverse expressions of service, creating a cooperative purpose for the team.

2. What are my priorities? That is, those matters in life you consider most important not just in word but in work behavior as well. How do your calendar and bank statement reflect these priorities?

Think of your priorities as the spiritual drivers for the "why" of what you do. Priorities determine who gets your attention and other resources and when. They are your strategic metrics for why you invest yourself. For example, faith may be a priority for you so you invest attention in worship and small groups weekly. You attract relationships at work with others who have a similar emphasis on faith.

By investing yourself in others according to your priorities, you encourage them. They sense the high value you place on your relationship with them and are attracted to you. Such encouragement is the relational glue that bonds you together as a team.

3. What is my unique contribution to make in the world through my work, and how do I live into it daily?

Core values are the "how" that equip. Priorities are

"why" that encourage. Think of your unique contribution as "what" you do that edifies. It is driven by your core values and priorities and the manifestation of what you understand to be your created purpose.

As you redefine reality in the negative world and achieve your spiritual dreams, you act to deliver your unique contribution and edify others. Paul sees your positive results at work serving to help others see, learn, and grow into a maturity that approaches that of Christ. Such edification is the spiritual wind beneath the wings of your work, creating a lift and leverage that glorifies God and drives your work with a fresh breeze of meaning and satisfaction.

Just as "birds of a feather flock together," so you literally attract people with whom you share core values and priorities and those to whom you can contribute uniquely. This attraction factor is a key determiner for how you conceive a Faith Positive lifestyle with others, whether on your team or with customers walking through your doors. By focusing on the positive and filtering out the negative, you choose whom you attract. Your faith and how you work with greater joy are the magnetic predispositions for converging relationships with those people with whom you best conceive.

For example, if you conceive your work more positively because you choose to focus and filter in this way, you attract positive people. Those who resonate on this frequency are literally drawn to you because of your common core values and priorities pitch and the relevance of your unique contribution to their spiritual growth needs.

Conversely, if your work life is more negative, you find people coming into your business relationships who are more negative themselves. They vibrate on a negative pitch and are drawn to you on that frequency.

You attract and cooperate with others. You resemble those with whom you share common core values and priorities who will receive your unique contribution whether as customers, team members, or vendors. Sometimes you may attract those you don't want to attract.

Do you ever find yourself complaining about your customers? They don't pay their bills on time, or maybe they're constantly trying to get something for nothing.

Who attracted them?

What about your team? Ever hear yourself saying something like, "You just can't find good help these days," or "Nobody wants to work anymore"?

You volunteered for this mission, right?

Think about your suppliers or vendors for a moment. Do you refer to them as "always having a hand in your pocket" or "wouldn't cross the street to help me"?

Who chose to do business with them?

Ask yourself: "How am I attracting these people? What is there about me—my core values, priorities, and unique contribution—that attracts them?"

Mike called to thank a friend who regularly sent potential customers to his business. He said, "Everyone you refer is so positive and friendly."

"That's because," she said, "I go out of my way to find positive and friendly people to do business with."

Mike wanted all the new business he could get, but at what cost? He made a quick and easy decision. He decided the more he became the type of person he wanted his customers to be, the more he would attract those customers and even his team. His friend's positive referrals conceived with him a Faith Positive business.

One of the greatest challenges to conceiving a Faith Positive lifestyle is understanding that like attracts like. Like Mike, you choose your customers, team, and vendors. They are in your work life because you drew them to your business. You attracted them by way of your core values, priorities, and unique contribution.

Ponder Your Faith Positive Work for a Moment #FaithPos

List your core values.

Write down your priorities.

Put down on paper your unique contribution to the world.

Make a list of people with whom you share some of the above.

Once you perceive your work life as positive, then you begin to attract others who share your positive direction. Team members and customers who choose to increase faith with greater joy at work so they love God and others more find their way to you. It's a documented reality that you are like those with whom you choose to be.

In 1948, Boston University and a research team began a heart disease project searching for indicators that predict heart attacks. More than twelve thousand persons from three generations have participated. The results are fascinating not only in predicting heart attacks but also in proving the undeniable nature of how you attract others.

Obesity is a direct correlative to heart attacks. The Framingham Heart Study found that obese people attract one another, and if you are not obese but associate with obese persons, you are about 171 percent more likely to become obese yourself.

Think about it. Associating with individuals who have unhealthy eating habits creates the context in which your nutrition behavior changes. The attraction factor not only draws those with whom you share similar traits; it changes the physical characteristics of those attracted.

Divorce is a major life stressor. Researchers studying the effects of divorce on heart attacks also discovered that if you socially associate with mostly divorced persons, you are about 147 percent more likely to divorce yourself.

Think about it. If you work in an office with people who chronically complain about their spouses, or ex-spouses, pretty soon your view of your spouse becomes jaundiced. You see what you're looking for. It doesn't take long for you to become impatient with your spouse's shortcomings and look for greener grass on the other side of the bed rather than staying home and fertilizing your own.

Your spiritual responsibility and privilege are to attract positive teammates, vendors, and customers with whom to do business as a Christian.

Ask for Hope That Helps

It's also up to you to let go of any need you might have to do all the work yourself, thinking it's easier for you to do it yourself than to involve others. Complete cooperation in this conceive core practice is rooted in the reality that like the farmer and his extraterrestrial secret, you are to put together your spiritual dream puzzle with others.

As Paul puts it, we "[grow] and [build] . . . up in love, as each part does its work" (Eph. 4:16, NIV). When you conceive a Faith Positive lifestyle, you expect and accept help from others.

When Dr. Joey's older daughter was two, "I do it, Daddy" was one of her favorite statements. She would say it and then try to open a door, even though she could hardly reach the knob.

Sometimes she couldn't do what she attempted. She would keep trying until she became so frustrated her words of "Help me, Daddy" came out, "Hope me, Daddy."

As you learn to increase your faith with greater joy at work, you'll attempt something you think you can do on your own. "I do it," you'll say. But then you will get frustrated and realize that you could use the hope that help brings. That's when you transform your work style to a positive one by intentionally attracting positive team members.

Asking for hope helps draws to you other hopeful people who are willing to help. All things in your work become possible as your team huddles around you, calling plays the negative forces in the world are defenseless against. You gain much-needed information about your work's frozen blue chunks and anything else that is a knowledge deficit. You recall that you were cared for in ways you forgot.

Increase your faith with greater joy at work so you love God and others more and attract those with whom you can redefine your reality, conceive your Faith Positive lifestyle, and make your spiritual dreams come true.

Ponder Your Faith Positive Work for a Moment

#FaithPos

Name one person you can ask for help at work.

Grab and *Go*

As you start to cooperate completely, conceive with others these positive thoughts:

1. No matter how well you perceive your work life, there is always something you miss, like the farmer and the chemistry professor.

2. When you're "of the world," you waste time and energy pulling on your own bootstraps.

3. Define your core values, priorities, and unique contribution to make to the world. You attract customers, teammates, and suppliers with whom you share these qualities.

4. Equip, encourage, and edify others.

5. Ask, "Hope me" and "Help me."

.

CHAPTER 5

Compare and Compete Rarely

"Love never fails."

—1 Corinthians 13:8, NKJV

A duck hunter in town was said to have the best retriever in the county, but he refused to take anyone hunting with him to see the dog work. Finally he agreed to let one friend go duck hunting with him. He made the fellow promise not to tell anyone in town about his dog.

The friend promised, and so off they went duck hunting. He shot a duck, and the dog took off to retrieve the downed bird. Instead of swimming, the dog walked on the water to the downed bird, picked it up, and returned it, still walking on the water, to the hunters.

The owner of the dog turned to his partner and said, "Now do you understand why I don't want you to tell anyone in town about my dog?"

"Yes, I do," the fellow replied. "I wouldn't want anybody to know I owned a dog that couldn't swim, either."

So, how do you conceive with others at work—a dog that walks on water?

Or a dog that can't swim?

Dogs That Don't Swim

One of the largest challenges you face doing business in the negative world is attracting positive people with whom to conceive. As you discovered in the previous chapter, you attract those who resonate with your core values, priorities, and unique contribution. Your work amplifies this attraction factor. If you worry negatively, you find yourself partnering with similar folks who are of the negative world—an ego-driven, compare-and-compete reality.

How Much Personal Power Do You Give to Drowning Dogs?

The reality is you become negative at times. It happens on this side of heaven. However, you have a choice about how much personal power you give away to negative people as you conceive your Faith Positive lifestyle.

Work is where you truly discover the kind of persons you have attracted. Positive people encourage you to recover when you fall, remind you that mistakes are expected, and help you back up onto the Faith Positive highway. Negative people discourage you by saying, "Stay down," ridicule you for even trying, and drop you over a cliff of despair.

You have attracted negative people into your work life at some point. You know their names.

Regardless of their actual names, I call them Eeyore Vampires.

You remember Eeyore from Winnie the Pooh. Whenever Pooh, Tigger, or Piglet suggested some wonderfully positive play-day activity for Christopher Robin, Eeyore's standard response was, "It'll never work."

The real challenge for you as a businessperson is that the Eeyore Vampires you work with or do business with aren't just cuddly characters from a children's book. They may be annoying as Eeyores by day, but actually they become vampires at sunset. They suck all the time, energy, and attention you allow.

At night they disturb your sleep with worry, which is nothing more than your imagination on negative steroids, and zap your energy for the next workday.

At night they call your home and distract your attention away from your family who, though they may be the most patient people in the world, become exhausted by the intrusions.

At night, they take your time by . . . You fill in the blank here.

You know these Eeyore Vampires.

You wish they would just go away.

You know they won't.

The question for you becomes, How much power will you give these Eeyore Vampires to conceive with you?"

What about your teammate who expresses his opinion about you with regular negativity to coworkers? How much time do you give to recovering your relationships with the other employees?

Or, what about the negative customer who throws a wet blanket on everything you try to do to please her with excellent customer service? How much energy do you waste on "she who won't be pleased"?

Or, what about the supplier who tells all the other competing vendors that you exclusively do business with him, preventing you from receiving the best bids? How much attention does he get?

Do You Compare and Compete?

The real challenge is when you allow Eeyore Vampires to have a negative influence on you and you begin to compare and compete. When you compare and compete, you embrace a scarcity mind-set that says: "There is not enough to go around in the universe. I got mine. You get yours." Business, life, and everything and everyone else become about you.

How much more love do you have for God and others when everything is about you?

Paul says not much when writing to the Corinthians about love. He says the compare-and-compete, Eeyore-Vampire mentality is the opposite of love. Such a negative relationship:

- struts.
- has a swelled head.
- forces itself on others.
- is always "me first."
- flies off the handle.
- keeps score of the sins of others.
- revels when others grovel.

Are you feeling the love? Hardly.

This negative view is the opposite of how God wants you to love others more. The conceive core practice is about abundance, that working together we can achieve more than any one of us alone. To cooperate is to acknowledge that like the flowers of the field and the birds of the air, there is more than enough to go around for all.

You compare and compete as you associate with Eeyore Vampires. You compare what you have and who you are with others. If you perceive you are behind the others, whether in your address, your kid's scored goals in soccer, or your vehicle's size, you compete with them to get more—more of whatever metric you negatively judge yourself.

Inevitably you assume a superior-inferior relationship. Rather than embracing the creative diversity and its abundance that's natural to the God-created universe, you conceive with negativity. You say, "Since I can accumulate more than you, I am a better person than you." You compare and compete in an effort to prop up your fragile ego. You allow Eeyore Vampires the power to reverse the osmosis of your perceiving filter so you filter out the positive and allow the negative to pass through. Rather than win, love stinks.

One of Mike's key responsibilities as an executive was to inspire, coach, and develop business owners. He worked for a company that weekly distributed reports with key sales data to help these owners have a sense of those areas of success and where they needed help. The reports weren't individual. They were territory-wide. Each owner received a report comparing personal results against everyone else's.

Compare-with and compete-against one another ruled. It inspired some to "beat" their fellow owners with more sales. It left others defeated and depressed knowing they didn't "stack up" well.

The corporate illusion was that the territory-wide reports made a positive difference. The weekly routine continued. Mike discovered the compare-and-compete results were anything but positive.

For those who took the information and always used it to have one more sale than everyone else, they limited themselves to a false goal of beating the competition. They thought they were winning, but in reality they were imprisoned by their competitors and doing one more sale than them. Their definition of success was tied to numbers instead of the customers they served.

The other group of owners found the information negative and depressing. They said to themselves, "I can't keep up with those at the top. Something is wrong with me." As hard as Mike tried to spin the reports in positive ways with these owners, the results were always the same.

Many owners choose to be chained to the compare-and-compete reports. But some have discovered a freedom from this imprisonment and realized an abundant path, freeing them to love God and others and increase faith with greater joy at work by finding the perfect ways to love those they serve and their team.

Which owners are you like? Do you give away your power to Eeyore Vampires who choose to compare and compete? When you do, you decrease your faith, let them steal your joy at work, and lessen your love.

> ## Ponder Your Faith Positive Work for a Moment #FaithPos
>
> What Eeyore Vampire habits fly around in your work right now?
>
> How do they limit and imprison you from the positive success you desire?
>
> What will you do to change those habits to free you to serve others and find more joy doing it?

A Better Way to Work

There is a better way to work than to compare and compete based on a negative, scarcity model. A way that increases your faith with greater joy at work so you love God and others more.

Dr. Wayne Dyer told *Success* editor Darren Hardy a story about newspaper columnist H. L. Mencken. He wrote some columns that engendered a number of negative letters from his readers. In response Mencken wrote a column that basically said this: "I have your letters that are critical of my recent columns in hand. I am holding them while sitting in the smallest room in my home. Soon they will be behind me."

Rather than give away his power to Eeyore Vampires, Mencken chose a better way. He detached himself from the negativity with a firm boundary and chose to cooperate completely.

It's so easy to waste time, energy, and attention worrying about what others think and allow them to form your filter in negative ways. When you buy what they sell, you are complicit in this conspiracy by giving away the perceive and conceive core practices of your Faith Positive lifestyle.

The better way is to seek out teams of positive people. Like Mencken, deny the negative people your positive time, energy, and attention. Put them behind you. Remember when Jesus said to Peter, "Get behind Me, Satan"? (Luke 4:8, NKJV).

So, how do you live into this Faith Positive relationship orientation so you increase faith with greater joy at work? Let's say you walk up on a negative conversation in the break room among some Eeyore Vampires. One is talking negatively about whatever she can imagine.

A Faith Positive first response is to redirect the conversation. Take it in a completely opposite direction by saying something like, "I sure am glad my kids got back to school after that snowstorm." Your goal is to diffuse the rampant negativity of the conversation by introducing a completely new subject.

If the Eeyore Vampire resumes the negative tirade, next attempt to reframe the conversation. Let's say she attacks the owner: "He's never done anything right," and "I'm not really sure how he keeps the company afloat."

Reframe the conversation by piggybacking your remarks onto hers and say something like, "Well, I know what you mean. He's certainly not perfect. And yet every paycheck he's ever written me cleared the bank." You reorient the polarity of the conversation from negative to positive, while remaining on the subject.

When your efforts to redirect and reframe fail, the third step to dealing with this Eeyore Vampire without becoming one yourself is to remove yourself as quickly as possible. See the Eeyore Vampire as if she has the flu and is sneezing all over the break room, infecting everyone in it. Negativity is just as infectious as the flu. Maybe more so.

Remove yourself immediately from personal contact.

Then do the Dr. Joey Two-Step developed from Mencken's response. These are steps because they work best in a sequence, like the three above, and also because you are stepping away from the Eeyore Vampire.

First, grab the handle. (Mencken was sitting in the smallest room in his home, remember?) Imagine the handle as your answer to, What can I learn from this situation and the Eeyore Vampire?"

What lesson can you learn from this Eeyore Vampire

that will increase your faith? Create greater joy at work? Help you love God and others more?

The second step in Dr. Joey's Two-Step: Flush!

What do you flush? The negative emotions, thoughts, and any other dimension of the interaction that may become Velcro for you. Be patient with yourself as your mind wanders back over the experience. Yet be brutal in your flushing. Some negative encounters require multiple flushes to rid yourself of the lingering effects.

As you compare and compete rarely, using these Eeyore Vampire-slaying strategies, you give yourself permission to increase your faith with greater joy at work as the unique person you are, and you free others to do the same. As they pursue positivity in business with you, together you step away from the scarcity mentality of compare-and-compete and embrace your created nature of cooperation. Both of you are winners!

You truly love God and others in the way Paul describes. You:

- never give up.
- care more for others than for self.
- take pleasure in the flowering of truth.
- put up with just about anything.
- always look for the best.
- never look back.
- trust God always.

Compare and compete rarely so you love God and others more and attract those who choose to cooperate completely. Now you are ready to conceive positivity at work on the ultimate level—collaborating with others.

Grab and *Go*

As you compare and compete rarely, remember:

1. The "dogs" you work with either walk on water or can't swim.

2. You have a choice about how much power you give to Eeyore Vampires.

3. Eeyore Vampires embrace a scarcity mind-set based in the negative world that says: "There is not enough to go around in the negative world. I got mine. You get yours." Positive people work from an abundance mentality of, "There is more than enough to go around."

4. Slay Eeyore Vampires:

    • Redirect the conversation.

    • Reframe the conversation.

    • Remove yourself from the conversation.

5. Do the Dr. Joey Two-Step:

    • Step 1: Grab the handle.

    • Step 2: Flush!

CHAPTER 6

Collaborate with Others

"If you handle the work this way, you'll have the strength to carry out whatever God commands you, and the people in their settings will flourish also."

—Exodus 18:23

Y ou increase your faith as you share core values and priorities through Faith Positive teams, as you encourage one another's unique contributions to the world with greater joy at work. You create habits from this conceive core practice so you love God and others more as you intentionally filter out the Eeyore Vampires and focus on cooperating with positive people with complementary abilities. You avoid attracting the ones who say, "It'll never work," and discover instead the ones who equip, encourage, and edify. This kind of team manifests an abundant life: Faith Positive at the ultimate level—collaborating.

You Choose

You choose the people with whom you collaborate—the customers, team, and suppliers. One of the challenges is accepting that others really do want to help you. You have everyone you need to succeed positively, to collaborate and increase your faith with greater joy at work so you love God and others more.

A young son and his dad were walking through the woods one day. They approached a large rock, and the little fellow said, "Hey Dad! Do you think I can lift that rock?"

"Of course you can," the dad said, "if you use all your strength."

The boy squatted down over the rock, put his hands around it, took a deep breath, and pulled on it as hard as he could. He failed to budge the rock even one inch.

Then he took an even deeper breath and pulled on the rock even harder, grunting with all his might. Still the rock did not budge.

"I thought you said I could move this rock," the son said as he stood up next to his dad.

"I did," the father replied, "but you didn't use all your strength."

"Yes, I did," he said. "I gave it all I had."

"You could have asked me for help," the dad said.

Can you relate with the boy? Tried to do the work alone before and thought you were using all your strength?

Moses tried to go it alone. After surviving the crossing of the Red Sea and other death-defying acts, the Hebrews worked to figure out what life was like post-Egyptian slavery. As their fearless leader, Moses tried answering all their questions about God, judging between neighbors, and teaching God's law and instructions. So the people lined up from morning to night, waiting to talk with Moses.

Moses' father-in-law, Jethro, came by for a visit and observed this waiting-room-only leadership challenge. As only a father-in-law can, Jethro said to Moses: "This is no way to go about it. You'll burn out, and the people right along with you. This is way too much for you—you can't do this alone. . . . Let me tell you how to do this *so that God will be in this with you.* . . . You need to keep a sharp eye out for competent men . . . and appoint them as leaders over groups. . . . They will share your load and that will make it easier for you. If you handle the work this way, you'll have the strength to carry out whatever God commands you, and the people in their settings will flourish also" (Exod. 18:17–23; emphasis added).

Like the little boy and Moses, you have everyone you need to succeed positively, to collaborate and increase your faith with greater joy at work so you love God and others more. The strategic pivot for you to make as you conceive your Faith Positive lifestyle is this: God is in this with you.

Remember how you've been in a carpool since your birth? God sends positive people—faith-filled, joyful, and loving—with whom you collaborate as a team, rooted in your core values, priorities, and unique contributions.

As you kick the Eeyore Vampires to the curb, your mantra becomes, "It costs too much to do business with some people." Those people are the ones who expect you to do it all. Like Jethro told Moses, "This is way too much for you—you can't do this alone." Collaborate with others God sends to you to increase faith with greater joy at work so you love God and others more.

Knowing Them When You See Them

You know what it's like to burn out and to do the work of several people as Moses did. You're probably asking, "But how do I recognize these people God sends to collaborate with me at work?"

You can know when you see them. Jesus put it this way: "I am the Vine, you are the branches. When you're joined with me and I with you, the relation intimate and organic, the harvest is sure to be abundant. . . . This is how my Father shows who he is—when you produce grapes, when you mature as my disciples" (John 15:5–8).

The way you know the people with whom you best collaborate is first to ensure you are joined with Jesus intimately. Remember those ten minutes in the morning and in the evening in which you perceive the positive? Those few minutes create an organic relationship of connectedness. You grow with Jesus. Again, you are not alone but have a team-building Partner within you to whom others are attracted.

Next, you know them when you see them by their mature fruit. They produce fruit which you inspect and discern.

What kind of fruit? Here are five key characteristics to look for in people whom you attract and with whom you want to collaborate. Of course you have position descriptions to guide you in the technical aspects of collaboration at work. Think of these as the off-the-resume qualities, the mature fruit you want on the team to grow a Faith Positive lifestyle.

Listen

The first mature-fruit characteristic is they listen.

A line in the movie *Pulp Fiction* goes something like this: "Are you really listening or just waiting to talk?"

Mike decided to hire a new team member after interviewing her numerous times. After several months of training and coaching, this new team member wasn't doing the job she was hired for—selling products to new and existing customers. They mutually agreed that Mike would help her find employment elsewhere.

On her final day they discussed her refusal to sell as she was hired to do. Mike reminded her that during each of the interview sessions they had, he told her, "This is a sales position."

She smiled and said, "Oh, I never listened to what you said in the interviews. I just needed a job."

Self-absorption is a symptom of a compare-and-compete lifestyle. Listening to another to the point of understanding is one of the hallmark qualities of someone who bears mature fruit, with whom you best collaborate in a Faith Positive lifestyle. Such a person refuses any claim to know all the answers to your business questions without consultation. Instead they seek out mutually beneficial knowledge. They ask rather than assume.

People with whom you can enjoy the Faith Positive lifestyle in a collaborative relationship listen to understand.

Ponder Your Faith Positive Work for a Moment   #FaithPos

Remember an occasion in which you listened to someone and your work benefited. Call or write that person right now and express your gratitude.

Humility

A second mature-fruit characteristic of these people with whom you team to increase faith with greater joy at work is humility. Humble people understand how collaborative, Faith Positive relationships work. When thrust into the limelight, they speak of others and their contribution to achieving the impossible and talk about how much fun it was. They redefine reality to include the team who fulfilled the dream.

You can see such humility in NASCAR racing. The drivers are the real celebrities in this sport, making millions of dollars running cars and endorsing everything from soft drinks to motor oil. The drivers make the headlines and show up on a cereal box. You can probably name at least one of these drivers, but can you name a tire changer? You see, while all this high-profile, big-money activity is going on, down in the pits is a team of guys who aren't asked to endorse anything. They'll never get their faces on anybody's box of cereal. This team works together to change tires, fill gas tanks, make track-bar adjustments, and clean windshields, or else the driver is dead on the track.

As it is with that driver, so it is with you at work. You are on a team of people helping the business go around daily. Those who are humble can name all these teams and do so at every opportunity. Humble people use words like *we* and *us* and *the team*.

Ponder Your Faith Positive Work for a Moment   #FaithPos

Name one team of people who keep your business on track. Call or write them to say thank you.

Mutual Benefit

A third mature-fruit characteristic of persons you attract and choose to collaborate with are on the team to achieve mutual benefit. They share accomplishments, both the credit and the rewards. They genuinely don't care who gets the credit as long as the team benefits.

Dr. Joey really doesn't like squirrels so he bought a bird feeder called "The Absolute." The Century Tool & Manufacturing Co. of Cherry Valley, Illinois, made it with a counterweight device that shuts the feeder door when anything heavier than a bird lights on it. When it first came on the market, Sue Wells, director of the National Bird-Feeding Society, says she and others thought someone "had finally come up with the ultimate solution."

Based on Dr. Joey's personal observation along with Sue and others, squirrels have defeated this most ingenious device by teaming up for mutual benefit. While one squirrel stands on the counterweight bar behind the feeder, keeping the front door from shutting, the other squirrel stands on the roost and feeds. Then they switch places.

These squirrels understand mutual benefit. They work with greater joy for everyone's mutual benefit. If squirrels can do it, maybe you can, too.

People with whom you want to collaborate choose mutual benefit for all involved. It is a core value that guides their priorities and drives the unique contribution they offer as they are in the negative world but not of it. Mutual benefit is a mature fruit within those you want to attract, choose, and invite onto the team to collaborate.

> **Ponder Your Faith Positive Work for a Moment**   #FaithPos
>
> Who is someone with whom you have enjoyed a mutual benefit?
>
> What role does this person serve on the team?
>
> Call or write that person and offer your thanks for a specific experience. Invite them to invest more deeply in your Faith Positive work.

Accountability

A fourth mature-fruit characteristic of people with whom you desire to collaborate for greater joy at work is that they hold you accountable. They bring out the best in you by asking questions that force you to be surgically honest with yourself. Such questions avoid embarrassing or humiliating you and create a healthy amount of pressure that pushes you into those habits and patterns that shape your positive success.

Think about it this way. You have a rubber band in your hand. It lays there in a certain shape. You pick up the rubber band and stretch it out and around a stack of cards. The band has changed its shape in response to the stack of cards and the pressure you put on it to fit. As long as it is around the cards, the band maintains that shape. Relieve the pressure by taking it off the cards, and what happens? It goes back to its original shape.

You are like that rubber band. You need accountability built into your collaborative relationships to conceive a Faith Positive lifestyle. The give-and-take, the encouragement to do and be better, and the reality that this person with whom you collaborate depends on and benefits from your best efforts motivate this relationship. This pressure keeps you in tip-top shape, focusing on a Faith Positive lifestyle and filtering out the negative. As long as you are in this relationship, you take on a shape of increasing faith with greater joy at work so you love God and others more out of your core values and priorities while making your unique contribution. Remove the pressure of the relationship, and you goose-step your way back into the crowd of Eeyore Vampires who work in a compare-and-compete manner.

Ponder Your Faith Positive Work for a Moment   #FaithPos

Consider: Who is the person who puts healthy pressure on me to be at my best at work? How can you best express your appreciate to this person?

The Golden Rule

The fifth and final mature-fruit characteristic you look for in grafting your Faith Positive teams is they live out of the Golden Rule. They treat others the way they want to be treated—humble listeners who work for mutual benefit and keep others accountable. The Golden Rule is the foundation of collaborative relationships.

You definitely know people with whom you enjoy a Golden Rule relationship. However, you probably have thought of some folks who possess anything but these characteristics. Perhaps you see them as more than Eeyore Vampires; you see them as your enemies.

Remember—what you resist persists. Simply telling yourself, "I shouldn't be thinking about these enemies" causes your mind to focus on them even more.

Rather than criticizing yourself for thinking of these folks as enemies, look at them differently. Be grateful for your enemies.

Yes, that sounds counterintuitive, but think about it for a minute. What if, instead of demonizing them, you interpret your experiences with them as opportunities to bring out the best in you?

How? You dislike in others what you dislike about yourself. We all do.

So if an enemy has a certain core value or priority that really bothers you, ask, "Why is that?" Could it be that you see your own core value or priority reflected back? Or do you struggle with the temptation to work that way and don't like that about yourself?

Mike was dealing with an enemy. He agonized over this person's next attack with every waking thought. Joy at work was replaced with anxiety and fear every time the phone rang. His nightly prayers revolved around begging God, "Make _____ leave me alone!"

For two years Mike begged until one night he asked God, "Will there ever be any relief?"

God's response was: "Love your enemies. Let them bring out the best in you, not the worst. . . . If all you do is love the lovable, do you expect a bonus? Anybody can do that" (Matt. 5:44, 46).

The last thing Mike wanted to do was to love and pray for his persecutor. Yet his persecutor was a child of God, too. Maybe this person was going through a difficult time, maybe an illness or some other significant life event.

As Mike began to see the individual who like himself was doing the best he could with what life brought him, God whispered, "You may be the only one who prays for this person today."

Mike's prayers transformed from "Is there any relief?" to "Please bless with your love." After only a few days of praying for blessings instead of relief, Mike's prayer time actually became fun. He saw God was building a more positive, powerful relationship between them. Joy returned in his work as this person became friendly. He increased his faith with an infusion of joy at work that allowed him not only to love God in a greater way but to love this enemy as well.

Redefine your reality about your enemies so you can

fulfill your spiritual dreams as Mike did. Sure, you most likely won't choose to be in a Faith Positive, collaborative relationship with this Eeyore Vampire; he reflects back to you negativity that's of the world.

Yet what have you really done if you return negativity for negativity? Simply multiplied the Gross Negative Product around you, sending out more negative vibrations that attract more negative people as customers, teammates, and suppliers whom you classify as enemies . . . and the cycle perpetuates.

Ponder Your Faith Positive Work for a Moment   #FaithPos

Name one enemy whom you find challenging to love. Breathe a silent prayer, asking Christ to transform your attitude toward this person.

Jesus wants you to see this person's negative behavior as the opposite of how you choose to increase faith with greater joy at work. Use it to keep yourself accountable. Let them bring out the best in you, which is the ultimate investment in your positive success, making you more intentional about loving God and others more through collaborative, mature-fruit relationships.

Celebrate the humble listeners who work for the mutual benefit of all and keep one another accountable in golden ways. These God-sent people collaborate with you to conceive a Faith Positive lifestyle in the negative world.

Grab and *Go*

As you collaborate with others, remember:

1. "Are you listening or waiting to talk?"

2. Be humble enough to work on your organization's pit crew.

3. Squirrels work for mutual benefit. So can you and your team.

4. Spend time with those who keep pressure on you to fit a positive shape and bring out the best in you.

5. The Golden Rule works. Work the Golden Rule.

believe the positive in faith at work

Believe the Positive in Faith at Work

"He is not here; for He is risen, as He said."
—Matthew 28:6, NKJV

I t was one of those snows you remember for a long time when you live at the beach, large enough to make a huge snowman.

Dr. Joey, his wife, and almost three-year-old daughter did just that—rolling and piling snow into a six-foot snowman complete with ginger-snap eyes, carrot nose, stick arms, and chocolate-chip-cookie buttons. His daughter insisted the snowman wear a hat. And, of course, they named him Frosty.

Dr. Joey read her the story of Frosty and how he came to life one day as it snowed. So Frosty had to be his name.

As they finished Frosty and stood back to admire him, the daughter asked, "Daddy, when is he gonna come alive?" She remembered the story.

"I don't know, honey. We'll have to watch and wait," Dr.

Joey said.

How do you tell your daughter who believes in the magic of an old silk hat that it's not real?

The next day brought the same question: "Daddy, when is he gonna come alive?"

"I don't know, honey. We'll have to watch and wait," he said again, knowing that his answer wouldn't satisfy her the next day, but what else could he say? "Go ask your Mother?" would only get him in trouble.

The next day came and brought the same question, "Daddy, when is he gonna come alive?"

Dr. Joey had nothing.

But she was ready: "I know, Daddy. He comes alive when we're not looking."

Remind you of Someone else who came alive while no one was looking?

Do you believe that life wins over death despite the negative world?

If you want to increase faith with greater joy at work so you love God and others more, you better.

There is more to your work than meets the eye because what you think exists is based primarily on how you perceive reality. It is based on your experiences with others as you conceive and collaborate with positive people.

There is much more to your work than what you can control, manipulate, or even influence. Someone who redefines your understanding of reality with the miraculous breakthroughs you didn't see coming. Results that are bigger than life. Your faith increases as you believe and your spiritual dreams come true.

Your work is evidence there is more to business that comes alive when you aren't looking. God is at work in your work in ways that are beyond your ability to control, manipulate, and influence in the negative world.

You just have to believe, the emotional dynamic and third core practice of your Faith Positive lifestyle.

Ponder Your Faith Positive Work for a Moment #FaithPos

Remember a time when you questioned if your
work could come back to life? An experience of
discouragement on the job? And eventually your joy at
work returned. What was that like for you?

CHAPTER 7

Believe Your Birthright

"Now faith is the substance of things hoped for,
the evidence of things not seen."

—Hebrews 11:1, NKJV

God created you in the divine image and likeness. It's indelibly stamped in your spirit. You are like your Creator because you think (perceive), love (conceive), and are creative (believe). Work is your expression of creativity. It's how you "bear fruit and multiply" (see Gen. 1:28) as our spiritual ancestors, Adam and Eve, did. It's why work brings you joy.

Do you believe you can work and create positive results in faith with greater joy in the negative world? You were created to work, and at its best your work gives God glory. As it does, you realize God's cosmic activity is in play as you work collaboratively.

And that's when your faith increases. You expect God-sized activities with specific results you don't see yet (Heb. 11:1). Your faith grows as you increase in emotional confidence and believe that certain outcomes will manifest right before your eyes. Think of it as the faith reality.

You hold certain beliefs about your work—the people

you work with, your customers, how much money you make to financially provide for you and your family, etc. You emotionally invest your beliefs in your work based on your experiences. As accurate as your beliefs in this negative world may be, there is still much about your work that comes alive when you're not looking and surprises you.

This faith reality, a realm of work that defies description, makes it possible to increase faith with greater joy so you love God and others more even in a negative world. Otherwise what you think about and experience with others is all there is. Unfortunately that is negative for many of us much of the time. You've been there, done that, and collected all the logoed shirts, right?

The wonderful aspect of the believe core practice is that you can become aware of it, and through your work increase your faith with greater joy. You perceive and conceive the positive in a negative world, and you also believe your world comes alive when you're not looking—that spiritual resources beyond your ability to influence, control, and manipulate converge in miraculous ways. The intersection of you and God working together is faith reality.

Here's how it works. Two sisters walked into a Goodwill store in Danville, Virginia. They mainly browsed, and one sister found an attractive pearl necklace. She liked it, tried it on, and decided to buy it for 69 cents.

She returned home to Arizona where she wore the pearls and someone complimented her. She told her story to which the person responded, "Oh, I think they're worth more than 69 cents. You should have those appraised."

She did. The pearl necklace was valued at a little more than the purchase price of 69 cents . . . $50,000.

Your definition of reality misses the target sometimes. Reality gets redefined quickly. Resources beyond our ability to influence, control, and manipulate converge in unexplainable ways, and a faith reality emerges.

You define reality based on your best information and

interpretation of your experiences. This reality is rooted in mainly an outward appearance, those factors that are evident. The truth is that there is a reality beyond the obvious.

Dr. Joey's grandmother gave him and his brother a chocolate Easter bunny every year. They always looked forward to getting it, but there were some chocolate bunnies they liked better than others. They never really knew which chocolate bunny they had received until they bit into it.

Some years when they bit into the bunny, there was nothing but air inside. She gave them a hollow chocolate bunny.

Other years they bit into the chocolate bunny, which looked like the hollow bunnies, and discovered that she gave them a marshmallow-filled one. It was great because at least it had something inside besides air.

Their favorite years were those when they bit into the chocolate bunny that looked exactly like the hollow and marshmallow-filled ones and found that their grandmother gave them a solid chocolate bunny—chocolate all the way through.

They never knew which kind of bunny they had until they bit into it. Reality got redefined bite by bite. What appeared to be obvious changed quickly.

Ponder Your Faith Positive Work for a Moment   #FaithPos

What new habit will you develop to remind yourself daily to claim your birthright to believe with a solid, all-the-way-through faith?

You Were Born to Believe

Your version of work reality misses the target sometimes. There is much to working that you simply misunderstand. There is much more to team relations, customer satisfaction, and vendor contracts than you can see, hear, taste, touch, and smell.

You were born to believe that reality defies your description and experience. Like Dr. Joey's older daughter and her Frosty, you have had many similar experiences in which your business came alive when you were not looking. Resources converged in miraculous ways that you just didn't anticipate, and you call it a faith reality.

And yet, since our minds crave the familiar, believing in the faith reality is a challenge. It's not that the old dog can't learn new tricks. It's that you have to unlearn the old ones first.

As a child you carved out new neural pathways almost daily. From the moment of your birth, you imprinted people and experiences with a certain sense of awe and wonder over the many faces of reality. New experiences thrilled you because you were fascinated with life. You were like a sponge absorbing everything. Where did that childlike awe and wonder of adventure go?

For you to believe that you can increase faith with greater joy at work so you love God and others more in this negative world, you must reclaim your birthright to believe. You were born to believe in a faith reality. Hourly as a child you lived in and believed the reality that life is much more about what you misunderstand than it is about what you do. It is only as an adult you began to define your reality as what you can influence, control, and manipulate. Those same mental folders labeled "Familiar" shaped and formed your version of reality.

And yet as a Christian, you believe that faith is "the firm foundation under everything that makes life worth living. It's our handle on what we can't see" (Heb. 11:2).

Trusting God with what you can't see shapes what you believe and creates your faith reality, which determines how well you work with God. The way you believe your business comes to life, combined with how you perceive and conceive it, charts the course into positive success or poor failure.

Fortunately, the reality of how you believe in your Faith Positive lifestyle is far greater than what you know. Your perception is limited. Your conception is limited. You willingly suspend your disbelief to at least acknowledge that the borders of your faith reality are pretty close in. Based on appearances, your understanding of reality devalues those things worth much more, like inexpensive necklaces. Experiences you thought dead-ended come back to life with a faith reality you never dreamed possible. All things really are possible, you know. There is far more to your Faith Positive lifestyle than you ever imagine.

As a child you understood that there is a faith reality you cannot see but only glimpse, you cannot hear except in a whisper, you cannot taste but only sip, you cannot touch but just feather-brush lightly, you cannot smell but only catch a faint whiff. You believe in this faith reality, even if it only comes alive when you aren't there. You in faith believe and grow toward what you discover God doing around you. You trust God that you were born to believe.

You really don't know what positive success you can achieve until you claim your birthright to believe that you have access to God's infinite resources. Your perception and conception can create a lot more business than you imagine.

To achieve your spiritual dreams, you must believe and emotionally engage your work by increasing faith to a level of success you've previously left unexplored. The impossible becomes possible as you do. As you believe, you increase your faith and see God at work with you.

The prophet Habakkuk discovered this faith reality lies beyond the obvious appearances of the negative world, the impossible is possible, and you can believe and increase your faith. He confessed it this way:

"Though the cherry trees don't blossom and the strawberries don't ripen, Though the apples are worm-eaten and the wheat fields are stunted,

Though the sheep pens are sheepless and the cattle

barns empty,

I'm singing joyful praise to GOD.

I'm turning cartwheels of joy to my Savior God.

Counting on GOD's Rule to prevail, I take heart and gain strength.

I run like a deer.

I feel like I'm king of the mountain!" (Hab. 3:17–19; emphasis added)

The negative world would have you believe its rule prevails—that all there is to work is what you can see, like fruitless efforts and empty bank accounts.

When you believe, you increase your faith and count on "GOD's Rule to prevail"; the God who has cared for you since birth and still does today will achieve your spiritual dreams.

You were born to believe in this God-ruled faith reality of the Faith Positive lifestyle that is much greater than what you know. The day is coming when your faith increases more deeply, a miracle breaks through, and you ask, "How did that happen?"

God's rule prevails.

Believe it.

There is far more to the Faith Positive lifestyle than you ever imagine.

Ponder Your Faith Positive Work for a Moment   #FaithPos

Write a description of what your life will look like as you choose to increase faith with greater joy at work so you love God and others more.

It is your birthright to believe there is more capacity in your work and its ability to provide for you and your family than you've previously imagined. Every day you can claim this birthright as you choose to increase faith with greater joy at work so you love God and others more.

When you turn away from your birthright to believe—and we all do—you bend away from the positive God's rule of faith reality and toward your own ego. This distortion of your belief severely limits the positive success of your work and makes you negative.

Grab and *Go*

As you believe your birthright, claim these positive thoughts:

1. God created you in the divine image, and your work is the expression of divine creativity.

2. Your joy is greater at work when you redefine your reality to a faith reality.

3. God has far more valuable, available resources than you might imagine, like Goodwill pearl necklaces.

4. Believe your work is a solid-chocolate bunny business.

5. God's rule prevails even in a negative world.

CHAPTER 8

Bend Away from Ego

"With [you] this is impossible, but with God all things are possible."

—Matthew 19:26, NIV

While you probably don't remember it, you failed the first time you tried to walk. That's right, you fell down. Thankfully, you wore a diaper to buffer your bottom. You got up and kept trying until you stayed up on your wobbly legs.

You almost drowned the first time you tried to swim, didn't you? But you stayed in the water until you learned to trust it to support you.

Did you hit or kick a ball the first time you swung at it? You may have fallen flat on your backside, but you stayed after it until you made contact.

What about riding a bike? Remember skinning your knees and elbows, crying while your parent cleaned you up?

It takes a great deal of courage to keep trying in the face of failure. The natural human response is to give up, to find something else you're good at; to do only those activities in which you have demonstrated prowess rather than risk humiliation and embarrassment . . . again; to influence, control, and manipulate those things and people to conform to your standards of behavior or thinking or believing—your perfect reality, perfect because you're in charge.

Rather than believing in your birthright that work comes alive when you're not looking, you choose to exercise your ego and believe that you can do it on your own.

Warning Sign: Dead-End Ahead

Exercising your ego is the pathway to the dead end of your assumed perfection. It is assumed perfection because your egotistical logic runs something like this: "If I can just influence, control, and manipulate my customers, vendors, and teams, I will succeed. My work will run according to my schedule. I will accomplish my goals in my time. I will have everything I want. I will work harder, be more brilliant than my peers, and do more than anybody else. My business lifestyle will be perfect."

The self-made business professional lives negatively, restricted by the limitations of ego-driven choices, pursuing an assumed perfection that exists only as a fantasy, only a façade propped up by life *of* this negative world.

Avoid such self-made Eeyore Vampires as if they have a deadly disease.

Because they do.

Unfortunately you can't always avoid them.

Because sometimes you are one.

Does your own ego-driven, negative work prevent you from being successful? It is so easy to disbelieve that "with God all things are possible." That the means required for your accomplishing the impossible at work is always with you. As you disbelieve in faith reality, you bend your work into yourself, specifically your ego and the fantasized perfection. Work becomes merely about you and what you can do.

Think of it as economic navel gazing. You self-consume. The insatiable emotional appetite of your ego black-holes everything positive, spewing only negativity which interferes with your creating a Faith Positive lifestyle. These negative beliefs become:

Fears about finances—"The bank called. Surely they're not calling in my note because of a down month."

Suspicions about a team member—"He sure talks about our competition a lot. Could he be feeding them information?"

Mistrust of a vendor—"She says she's doing me a special favor with this contract. I have known her for ten years, but I wonder if she's telling the truth."

The dark, downward descent goes on and on.

These negative worries assault your ability to increase faith with greater joy at work. They cause you to bend further toward your ego in pursuit of that assumed perfection, or at least the skill to pull yourself up by your own bootstraps.

Ponder Your Faith Positive Work for a Moment #FaithPos

What or who are you trying to influence, control, and manipulate? Has it ever worked?

Business Will Be Better When . . .

So here you are at work, negative worries booming through your ego. You begin talking to yourself, and the conversation starts with, "I'll be OK. Business will be better when . . .

I get some new team members."

I find a new job."

I have more time."

I . . . "

Sure, you're important to your work. However, you are not the sum total of your work.

Jesus said it like this, "With man this is impossible . . ." (Matt. 19:26, NIV).

It appears you have to do it on your own, apart from God, when the economic noise assaults you at incredibly difficult decibel levels, and your first recourse is to bend in to your ego. You then set up unrealistic "perfect stages" of your work life when everything will be just right.

So what if those ideal scenarios you've dreamed about your business suddenly materialized? What do you picture then?

Do you see yourself working with God to coach, develop, and serve your customers and team? Or do you envision yourself after a year of rolling up your sleeves, at your company's next national convention seated next to the CEO, sounds of roaring applause ringing in your head?

Are you bent on serving others? Or toward your own ego?

Your ego fears failure, rejection, and a host of other paralyzing scenarios, none of which exist except in your emotions. This fear prevents you from getting up and doing what you can do, controlling what you can control, and avoiding worrying about the rest. This fear blocks from your heart the faith-reality that "with God all things are possible" (Matt. 19:26, NIV).

The way you work best is more about what you believe to be faith reality than you ever imagined. Maybe that's why you picked up this book, *Faith Positive in a Negative World*. You know the negativity of working *of* the world. You have exercised your ego to the point of exhaustion, trying to make something perfect out of your problems. You're hoping more is left in your work, more than what you and your ego have done so far. You're praying for an increase in faith and especially greater joy at work.

The good news is that there is much more to your work than what you've experienced so far. Remember that moment when you felt led to this work, to your unique contribution? Your excitement, passion, and desire to help others? Hope for that calling on your life to succeed peeks up through the cold adversity of your ego-constructed work like the first crocus of spring through six inches of snow.

Ponder Your Faith Positive Work for a Moment #FaithPos

What "perfect stage of your work" are you waiting for to be Faith Positive?

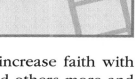

You were born to believe you can increase faith with greater joy at work so you love God and others more and generate success, avoiding bending inward to your ego. That's something you do to yourself when you allow the negative world to take over your emotions.

You are actually at your best, enjoying a Faith Positive lifestyle, when you live into your birthright to believe and imagine how you can best work to co-create with God a faith reality in a negative world. Let's discover how.

Grab and *Go*

As you bend away from ego, remember:

1. It takes a great deal of courage to keep trying in the face of failure.

2. Avoid Eeyore Vampires as if they have a deadly, communicable disease. Because they do. Unfortunately you can't always avoid them. Sometimes you are one.

3. Noisy worries assault your ability to increase faith with greater joy at work.

4. Does your own ego-driven, negative work prevent you from being successful?

5. Are you bent on serving others? Or toward your own ego?

CHAPTER 9

Best to Imagine

"God can do anything, you know—far more than you could ever imagine or guess or request in your wildest dreams! He does it not by pushing us around but by working within us, his Spirit deeply and gently within us."

—Ephesians 3:20

A friend traveled through Ireland with a tour group. They drove by bus through the beautiful countryside, admiring the rolling hills and green pastures.

She noticed that trees bordered the road. The more she looked at them, the more she realized that they were all planted and grown the exact distance apart. She asked her tour guide about the trees.

"Oh, yes," the tour guide told her. "Those trees were originally fence posts cut locally from trees. They were planted exactly five feet apart as fence posts. The soil is so rich here that the planted fence posts started sprouting limbs and eventually grew into trees again."

Would you have ever imagined that fence posts would come back to life?

Here's How It Works

You were born to believe, not bend toward your ego, so you can be at your best and imagine your work comes back to life in a Faith Positive lifestyle. Imagination is your pilot through the skies of faith reality. It is the jet fuel for increasing your faith with greater joy at work so you love God and others more. It propels you off the runway of the negative world and takes you into the stratosphere of believing that "with God all things are possible" as the tailwind of resources converges and sends you soaring.

Imagination is key to your Faith Positive success. You perceive, conceive, and believe based on more than what you alone can see, hear, taste, touch, and smell, and primarily on what you can imagine. "With God *all* things are possible." The unexpected happens. The unexplainable occurs. And you say, *All things really are possible.*

Your positive success is the culmination of how you think about it, partner with others to think about it, and then collectively imagine outcomes that seem unrealistic at the moment but are achievable as all of you believe in this faith reality. Paul describes it this way,

"God can do anything, you know—far more than you could ever imagine or guess or request in your wildest dreams! He does it not by pushing us around but by working within us, his Spirit deeply and gently within us" (Eph. 3:20).

It's best to imagine what God can do through the Spirit in you. A God-sized vision emerges from your creative imagination, beyond your wildest dreams, as his Spirit moves you to the moment and resources ready to achieve your spiritual dream.

These spiritual dreams often start small and grow large. You have picked up an acorn before and looked at it. It's about the size of a dime. Dr. Joey picked up an acorn under a 150-year-old oak tree on his farm. He stood there looking at the acorn, up at the tremendous oak, and wondered, "How did such a huge tree start as such a little acorn?" It defies all senses to understand or explain. You can only imagine.

Have you ever held a mustard seed in the palm of your

hand? It's about the size of a pencil point. You plant that pencil-point seed, and it grows into a six-foot-high bush. Who would have thought that was possible?

Jesus said that's all the faith you need, about the size of a mustard seed, to move mountains. When you believe all the imagination you need to do the impossible, to redefine your reality and achieve your spiritual dreams, is about the size of a mustard seed, you increase faith. Your joy at work soars. You love God and others more.

Rather than judging from appearances, Jesus sees the miracle in the small. Dr. Joey remembers his Great-Grandmother Frazier making yeast rolls. She would sift the flour and add the liquid and other ingredients. Then she would open a small packet of something magical called yeast. She dropped just a pinch or so in, an extremely small amount when compared with the flour. Next she would hand mix all of this concoction. Grabbing a handful of it, she would pat it out and put it down on the pan and let it sit.

"Grandma, what's it doing?" he asked.

"It's rising, son," she said.

"How?" he said.

"The yeast makes it rise," she told him.

How in the world does such a tiny amount of yeast make all that dough rise?

Your imagination is like yeast. When you are Faith Positive, believing that your work will succeed in ways that defy your logical understanding, you rise to achieve the faith reality time after time.

Ponder Your Faith Positive Work for a Moment   #FaithPos

Recall a time in your work when something small grew into something large. Did you see it coming? What did you think when it did?

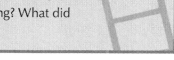

In a scene toward the end of an Indiana Jones movie, Indy is pursuing the Holy Grail, the cup Jesus drank from at the Last Supper. Indy has endured every kind of danger known to humanity, but he, his hat, and his bullwhip have made it through to this last test.

He stands on the edge of a bottomless pit. The pit separates him from the Holy Grail; yet he is close enough to see it. His clue indicates that if he believes, the way to the chalice will appear to him. Everything he sees tells him that he will plunge to his death should he step off the precipice.

Indiana Jones decides that he has come too far not to believe, so he closes his eyes, fully expecting to fall to his death, and yet he still takes that first step forward. When he does, much to his surprise, a bridge to the other side appears under his feet. Rather than dying, he runs across, seizes the cup, and returns safely.

The First Step Away Is the Hardest

Just as with Indiana Jones, that first step away from what you think you know to God's faith reality for your work is the hardest. The pull of the familiar ego, even though it's negative, is strong.

Mike meets his daughter at the gym each weekday morning. He cherishes the time spent with her, their conversations, and their shared enjoyment of exercise and fitness.

He faces one obstacle each day: his daughter likes to arrive at the gym at 4:45 am. That means Mike has to begin waking up around 3:50 AM. Once he's arrived, he's fine, but that first moment each morning he has to make the decision: "Do I roll over and keep sleeping? Or do I sit up, put my feet on the cold floor, and stumble into my gym clothes while gulping down a diet energy drink?"

Yes, that first step away is the hardest.

Your faith increases with greater joy at work so you love

God and others more when you believe that tiny acorns become huge oak trees, small mustard seeds become great bushes, and pinches of yeast make wonderful rolls. You positively succeed when you imagine that the first step you take away from what you know to what you believe causes the ground to rise up and support you. This first step is how you redefine your reality to God's faith reality and fulfill your spiritual dreams.

For your work to achieve its full potential, you imagine it at its best. As we've coached business executives, entrepreneurs, and owners through the years, we've discovered that the mundane minutia of working can consume most of your time, energy, and attention, leaving none for imagining possibilities beyond the current reality. Your imagination morphs into worry that God, who can do anything, is AWOL—that you've been separated permanently, mired down in the soul-sucking drudgery of what work can be.

Paul understands what it's like to know God more by absence than presence at work. As a tent-making evangelist, he suffered through being struck blind, shipwrecked, snake-bit, and stuck in prison among other experiences that must have caused him to wonder, "Now God, you called me to this work. And where are you?" And yet, from a prison, he writes his capstone epistle to the Romans and says: "Do you think anyone is going to be able to drive a wedge between us and Christ's love for us? There is no way! Not trouble, not hard times, not hatred, not hunger, not homelessness, not bullying threats, not backstabbing. . . . I'm absolutely convinced that nothing—nothing living or dead, angelic or demonic, today or tomorrow, high or low, thinkable or unthinkable—absolutely nothing can get between us and God's love because of the way that Jesus our Master has embraced us" (Rom. 8:35, 37–39).

When was the last occasion you and your team took some time away from the soul-sucking minutia to imagine your work at its best? To rekindle your beliefs that your work matters, that what you do makes a difference, that God has a definite purpose for your work—that a faith reality is the ultimate reality for business? That you can increase your faith with greater joy at work so you love God and others more?

Yes, God is inseparable from you.

Yes, your work might seem small, but Jesus sees it as miraculous.

Yes, God can do anything and sends his Spirit to work gently within you to join in the faith reality.

It is best to imagine your work in faith with joy and love.

Ponder Your Faith Positive Work for a Moment   #FaithPos

When was the last time you and your team took some time away from the soul-sucking minutia to imagine your work at its best? Reach out to Dr. Joey and Mike about how you can retreat to imagine your work at its best.

Grab and Go

Remember, it's best to imagine how you increase faith with greater joy at work so you love God and others more as you believe:

1. God can do anything, you know.

2. Acorns grow into sky-high oak trees.

3. Pencil-point mustard seeds grow head-tall bushes.

4. A pinch of yeast causes a pan of rolls to rise.

5. The ground rises up beneath your feet as you take that first step in faith.

achieve the positive in faith at work

Achieve the Positive in Faith at Work

"Ask and you'll get; seek and you'll find;
knock and the door will open."

—Luke 11:9

A woman drove down a heavily traveled street one afternoon after getting off work a little early. The radio was blasting her favorite song when suddenly her car quit. She managed to steer it over to the side of the street, got out, and looked under the hood.

An unfamiliar voice behind her said, "Lady, do you need some help?" She wheeled around to discover three young men standing behind her.

"Uh, no. Everything is fine," she said. "I'm calling AAA. They're on their way."

"You don't need to call anyone," one of the young men said, and grabbed her phone. The next thing she knew, she was on the ground, trying to cover her face and protect herself from the strong-armed blows pummeling her face first, then her stomach. Kick after kick broke her ribs. Blood oozed from her lips as she lost consciousness. No one saw anything as the three young men managed to start the vehicle and drove away.

A highly esteemed and successful businessman was being driven down that same street in his limo. His driver slowed down as he spotted the woman lying on the sidewalk in a pool of blood.

"Mr. James, there's a woman bleeding on the sidewalk over here. I'm going to get out and check on her," the driver said.

"No, you're not," Mr. James yelled back. "If I'm not at this meeting on time, I'll lose this deal. Drive on . . . now!"

"Can I at least call it in to 911?" the driver asked.

"Of course not," Mr. James said. "Then we'll have to waste time giving a statement. Turn left at the next intersection and take a back street to The Plaza."

A few minutes later an ethics professor from the local university stopped at the traffic light near where the woman was on the sidewalk, still bleeding. He peered through his windshield. "Is that a woman bleeding on the sidewalk?" he wondered. He slowly pulled away from the traffic light.

"It is, and she's bleeding a lot," he said out loud. "I'd better stop," and he slowed down to pull over.

"Wait a minute. Her attackers may still be around," he decided. He sped away, turning off the street, just in case the criminals were watching.

Just then a Latino construction worker pulled up to the traffic light. His beat-up work truck barely kept running while waiting for the light to change. He tapped out a backbeat on his steering wheel, glad to have the truck to himself so he could listen to his music.

He saw the woman lying on the sidewalk, checked the intersection, and pulled quickly over to the curb beside her. He jumped out of the truck and ran to her side.

"Hey lady! Are you OK?" he asked.

She only moaned and tried to cover her face.

"I don't have a cell phone," he told her. He stood there, then started pacing, trying to figure out what to do.

"Lady," he said, "I'm going to put you in my truck and take you to the hospital, OK?" And with that he picked up the woman in her blood-stained dress and gently placed her on the passenger seat, carefully shutting the door. He ran around to the driver's side, jumped in, and sped off down the street toward Mercy General.

Screeching in on two wheels, he pulled up to the Emergency Department door. He jumped out and ran in and screamed: "Somebody come help. A woman has been attacked."

Two attendants flew out the door, one of them screaming, "Bring a gurney and prep a room stat." They gingerly lifted the woman from the truck, placed her on the stretcher, and wheeled her inside.

The Latino construction worker followed closely behind, but when he tried to follow her through the trauma room doors, a loud voice stopped him: "Sir, I must talk with you first."

He pivoted over to the woman at the desk. "Sir, you must secure payment for our services before we can treat her. This is a private hospital, not one of the county facilities," she said.

Incredulous, the man said, "I just found her on the street. I don't know her."

"I'm sorry, sir," the woman continued. "Our rules are clear. You either secure payment now or take her somewhere else."

He straightened himself and said, "I will gladly pay for your services."

He pulled his wallet out and handed her his medical insurance card, not knowing how he would explain this to the boss, but knowing what he had to do.

"And here," he said, handing her his credit card. "Whatever else it costs that my insurance doesn't cover, you can put on my card."

Now which of these three—the businessman, the ethics professor, or the Latino construction worker—would you say works out of a Faith Positive lifestyle? Increases faith with greater joy at work so he loves God and others more?

Ponder Your Faith Positive Work for a Moment #FaithPos

Reflect on an opportunity you had recently in which you could have helped someone. Something simple is fine—opening a door for a mom with her arms full with a baby or an old man on a walker. What did you do? What could you have done?

The fourth core practice of a Faith Positive lifestyle is about how you achieve your spiritual dreams—how you can manifest all of the previous core practices of perceive, conceive, believe, and then achieve success while doing business *in* but not *of* a negative world. Consider this the physical dynamic of how you work with a Faith Positive lifestyle.

CHAPTER 10

Pay Attention to What's Most Important

"Give your entire attention to what God is doing right now."
—Matthew 6:34

O ver the years of coaching executives, entrepreneurs, and owners, we have observed something: When a child—"Johnny"—cannot seem to sit still in his school desk and focus, he's run through a battery of tests, labeled "ADD" or "ADHD" and medicated.

When Johnny graduates and grows up, sitting still at his desk long enough to finish an MBA, he is stuck in an office, surrounded by concrete and glass, and encouraged to multitask. Everything is now important to Johnny. So while he is conferencing with Asia, he is answering e-mail from a customer in Florida, sending a text to the vendor in Texas, completing a spreadsheet to present at a conference, and his wife is on hold, wondering if he will make it to his seven-year-old daughter's dance recital.

Is this how Johnny achieves positive success?

Does his faith increase?

What about his joy at work?

Does his daughter feel more love when he doesn't make it?

Is this a Faith Positive lifestyle?

Recent studies indicate that personal productivity diminishes precipitously with multitasking, as you divide your attention between too many sources, all clamoring for your focus. You get less done when you try to do more all at once.

But then you knew that.

Mike was interviewing a candidate, asking questions and taking notes. Deep in the conversation, almost out of nowhere, the candidate expressed her confidence that she was his best choice for the open position because she was good at multitasking. He put down his pen, slid an unrelated document across the table, and asked her to read what was on the document, while at the same time, recite her top three goals for the first year in this new position.

She was startled by the request and unsure of what to do. But there was one thing she did know for sure— there was no way she could read one document and recite something else simultaneously. Multitasking is a myth.

Ponder Your Faith Positive Work for a Moment   #FaithPos

Put a doodle pad beside your phone. Head a sheet "MT" for multitasking. Scratch a hash mark for each time you catch yourself talking on the phone and doing something else like reading e-mail, texting, working on a spreadsheet, etc. Track it for a week. Then track the next week and try to decrease the times you multitask.

To achieve your Faith Positive lifestyle, you focus and filter for positive thoughts or mentally pay attention to what is most important. You increase faith with greater joy at work so you love God and others more even though the negative world is filled with Eeyore Vampires telling you what should be important. The only way for you to achieve what others consider impossible, but what you believe can be done because you have perceived and conceived it, is to pay attention to what is most important. It's a matter of priority.

File that under "Easier Said than Done."

Your productivity quotient follows the 80/20 rule— about 20 percent of what you pay attention to on any given day contributes 80 percent to your productivity and revenue. Based on our experiences in coaching executives, entrepreneurs, and owners, the heavy dependence on technology-driven tools today pushes these percentages closer to 90/10.

Many business professionals today allow others to set the agenda with 24–7 access. Technology drives minutia on steroids to compete for attention, and all of it is "urgent."

If you truly want to redefine to the faith reality and achieve your spiritual dreams, you simply must pay attention to what is most important for you. Focus is the key to your productivity.

When Dr. Joey first started quail hunting, he got really excited when a large covey of birds flew up, thinking, *Wow! With that many birds flying, I can't miss!* He shot into the covey without really aiming at any bird in particular. He missed every time.

He learned to select one bird, focus his aim on that one bird in the covey, and shoot at that one bird. Most of the time, he downed it.

Focus is the key to productivity. Pay attention to what is most important and you achieve your spiritual dreams.

Jesus said it like this, "Give your entire attention to what God is doing right now" (Matt. 6:34).

Life Is Really Busy Today

Is there a difference between what you're doing and what God is doing right now?

Despite the fact that you have fast food, Keurig coffee, and same-day delivery, do you ever complete your to-do list? Perpetual coveys of tasks fly in your face.

How do you focus on one priority task—the most important—take aim, and fire away with your attention and increase faith with greater joy at work?

Just shooting into the covey of "urgent" items others put on your agenda?

At the end of the day, are you walking away shaking your head and asking, "What did I get done today?" hoping tomorrow slows down?

One of the more frustrating challenges to giving your entire attention to what God is doing right now is mentally being in the "right now." Your mind makes no distinction between yesterday, today, and tomorrow. You go there in a nanosecond. You are a time traveler as James Altucher describes in his book, *Choose Yourself.* You drift back to a previous experience and relive it in vivid colors, complete with rapid pulse and shortness of breath. Or you borrow from tomorrow, worrying about "what might be" should this happen or that occur.

So how is that working for you to increase your faith with greater joy at work? Are you finding more love for God and others?

Ponder Your Faith Positive Work for a Moment   #FaithPos

List all of the tasks that fly in front of you on a typical morning.

Put a check mark beside the ones that are most important.

Yesterday Is Gone—Tomorrow Will Be Faster

There's no going back to relive yesterday. Hoping tomorrow slows down so you catch up is a zero-sum strategy, also. Both decrease faith with less joy at work so you lose love.

Such an ill-founded hope sacrifices what is really

important to God in your work on the altar of what you think is important. God converges resources in a here-and-now moment, and you miss it. You give away to the negative world your power to choose what is important to God right now and neglect the faith reality of the present moment. Your spiritual dreams die.

When resources uniquely converge because the positive was perceived, conceived, and believed, someone will achieve because they acted in that present moment. Yes, someone will act on what is important and get outstanding results. They will focus on the one bird in the covey, take aim, fire, and hit the mark. They will pay attention to what is important because they have perceived it, conceived it with another, and believed it with their imagination, and they will achieve what everyone else considered impossible.

The question is, How will they know what is most important?

The most productive way to achieve your spiritual dreams is to pay attention to positive thoughts (perceive) and positive people (conceive) that God brings to your work as the Spirit works gently within you.

Pay Attention to God's Most Important

You probably have read this verse before: "Be still, and know that I am God" (Ps. 46:10, NKJV). To increase faith with greater joy at work so you love God and others more, put this verse on your makeup or shaving mirror, the dash of your vehicle, your computer's screensaver, and make PS4610 your smartphone's password. This single verse is the strategic key to physically achieving your spiritual dreams. Here's why:

"Be still . . ."

God respects your choices. Just as with Elijah and his depression-driven cave experience, God refuses to intrude on your noisy life and instead whispers in a still, small voice into your spirit. Select a whirlwind or fiery way to work, and God seems absent. Be still enough to listen, and God shows up strategically in a whisper, letting you in on the divine plan worthy of your entire attention. Your reality redefines to faith reality, and you achieve your spiritual dreams.

"*. . . and know . . .*"

How do you choose which most important positive thoughts and positive people to give your attention? How do you know?

Knowing God's plans drives your attention to priority positive thoughts and people. You know as you are still. Remember how you perceive with your ten minutes in the morning and ten more in the evening? That's how you know. You attract others as you are still. You gain courage to kick the Eeyore Vampires to the curb.

You increase faith with greater joy at work so you love God and others more when you know as you're still.

"*. . . that I am God.*"

The greatest impediment to achieving your spiritual dreams in the new faith reality is confusion over who gets your entire attention: God or you.

In our perceive core practice conversation, you discovered that you either pray (positive thoughts) or worry (negative thoughts). In our conceive discussion, you learned that you attract either positive people or Eeyore Vampires. In our believe chat, you found that you imagine (positive emotions) or bend in to ego (negative emotions).

To achieve your spiritual dreams, you choose who will guide your actions: God or you. Your choice determines your results: infinite success in faith reality or finite shortcomings of your own.

God is God and you are not.

Who gets more of your attention?

"Be still, and know that I am God" (Ps. 46:10, NKJV).

Ponder Your Faith Positive Work for a Moment   #FaithPos

Decide where you will put Psalm 46:10 so you see it often.

Then put it there.

Here are two strategies that our coaching clients find particularly effective to increase faith with greater joy at work while paying attention to what is most important.

1. *Ask God for Your To-Do List*

Who writes your to-do list? God or you?

Stephen Covey was fond of saying, "Schedule your priorities instead of prioritizing your schedule." He suggested that instead of allowing the negative world to determine your priorities and then shuffling those around, first discern your priorities and schedule among them.

You begin your day with five of your ten minutes spent perceiving positive outcomes to your scheduled appointments. Discerning and scheduling those appointments is an earlier activity for you to achieve.

End each week with some "be still" time. Eliminate any potential sources of distraction and meditate on what God is doing in your work. Ask God to give you insight on your activities for the next week. Seek God's movement in your work performance. Discern where God is leading and going and then prioritize your understanding. Create your to-do list and schedule it.

What strategies are you to implement? Whom are you to call? How are you to best approach both? God's to-do list is infinitely more resourceful, strategic, and prosperous than yours. It's of the faith reality of success.

"Be still, and know that I am God."

2. *Create Boundaries Around Technology*

The creep of technology intrudes into all our lives. As you pay attention to what is most important, you daily recognize the creep and create boundaries that limit it.

For instance, you're in a meeting. Your desk phone rings. Do you answer it? Do you read the Caller ID window and decide?

Let's say you're working on your computer on an important project. Is your e-mail open? Is it set on "automatic" so that it's making noises and popping up windows that interrupt your flow?

What if you're with a customer and your smartphone buzzes with a call? Do you take it?

Hopefully your answer is no in each case. At least sometimes, it's probably yes.

Create boundaries around your technology that allow you to focus completely on what is most important. You pay for technology services. They are to serve you, not vice versa. Here are three strategies to implement immediately:

• Use the "DND" (Do Not Disturb) function on your desk phone. If it's important, the caller leaves a voicemail you receive and answer at a strategically scheduled time.

• Uncheck the automatic updating of your e-mail on computers, tablets, and smartphones. Schedule specific times of day to check and answer e-mail.

• Turn off notifications for social media. Does paying attention to your friend's picture of her lunch increase your faith or create greater joy at work for you? You choose when to check your social media. If it's important to your business, someone is (or should be) tasked with that responsibility.

What Is Your Positive Life Trigger?

While you may agree with these strategies, what is your trigger for paying attention to what's most important to God? What motivates you and builds urgency for you in the faith reality so you do it?

Dr. Joey found his trigger one day as he stood by the open grave of a family member. The death was sudden and unexpected. As Dr. Joey stood there, his mind flooded with all the times he wished he had called just to say hi. And the unsent birthday cards. The unwritten "just because" notes. Dr. Joey cried . . . and decided he wasn't crying for the deceased family member but for himself. For the lost opportunities. The words left unsaid. The deeds left undone.

A beautiful dragonfly flew around the open grave, its iridescent wings glittering in the summer sun. Most dragonflies live only about a month.

As Dr. Joey stood at that open grave, staring at dragonfly, he wondered, "If I only had a month to live, what would I do?" Watching the sandy soil fill the grave and cover the casket, with dragonflies flitting about, he made a decision to live differently. To say all the words, some to people he hadn't spoken with in thirty years. To do for others now rather than waiting until later.

To pay attention to what is most important right now. To focus and filter for positive thoughts, avoiding just the familiar mental patterns. To go out of his way to find the unfamiliar because therein lies the faith-reality prize. To cooperate and collaborate with other positive people, comparing and competing rarely. To tolerate no Eeyore Vampires on Team Dr. Joey. To live into the birthright to believe and imagine the best in every opportunity God presents, steering clear of the bent to ego. To pay attention to what is most important to God, which leads to the achievement of spiritual dreams in this negative world—positive results like this book and the monumental transformation you're undergoing right now.

Like Dr. Joey, Mike has had times when he intended to do something and didn't. For instance, he wanted to go to the gym. But he didn't succeed on a consistent basis until he realized being with his daughter every day was his life trigger. He found his urgent focus in God's gift of his daughter.

What is your life trigger that creates an urgent focus on what's important to God? "Give your entire attention to what God is doing right now" (Matt. 6:34).

Ponder Your Faith Positive Work for a Moment   #FaithPos

Reflect on what you would do differently today if you discovered you had only thirty days left to live.

The Greatest Challenge

Your greatest challenge in paying attention to what is most important according to God is actually doing it and not just intending to do it. It's a lot easier to talk about paying attention to faith reality than it is to actually do it.

Intention is the road to nowhere.

How do you avoid this dead-end road?

Discover how in the next chapter.

Grab and *Go*

In a world that's constantly negative, remember to pay attention to what's important" and keep in mind that:

1. Multitasking to be productive is a myth. Ask Johnny.

2. Be still, and give your entire attention to God.

3. Yesterday is gone. Tomorrow will be faster.

4. Pay attention to what God is doing.

  • Ask God for your to-do list.

  • Create boundaries around technology.

5. What is your positive life trigger?

CHAPTER 11

Intention is the Road to Nowhere

"Fear nothing."

—Psalm 91:5

A business owner had two employees. He received a call from the cleaning service saying they could not get someone to the building to clean that week due to the snow.

The owner said, "We can do it." So he called one of his two employees into his office. "Tom, the cleaning service can't get here this week. So we're all going to pitch in and do a little cleaning. How about you clean the bathroom? All the supplies are in there."

Tom replied, "Boss, I really don't want to. My wife makes me clean the toilets at home, and I absolutely hate it."

Later Tom thought more about the owner's request and decided that if he could clean the bathroom at home, he could do it at work. It was not that big a deal. Besides, there was no shower at work. So he did it.

When Tom refused to clean the bathroom, the owner called Ralph, the other employee, into his office. "Ralph, the cleaning service can't get here this week. So we're all going to pitch in and do a little cleaning. How about you clean the bathroom? All the supplies are in there."

"Sure thing, boss. I'll be glad to," Ralph said.

Ralph never cleaned the bathroom.

Who would you want on your team—Tom or Ralph?

Ponder Your Faith Positive Work for a Moment   #FaithPos

When did you say no to someone and then went ahead and did it anyway?

And when did you say yes and decided not to do it?

A Story of Two Employees

Which one, Tom or Ralph, achieved positive results? Which one intended to?

Intentions—the stated desire of "I want to" or "I didn't mean to"—are pathways to your achieving positive results but not to be equated with achievement. "I want to" or "I didn't mean to" does nothing to change the outcome or the results. Intentions, by themselves, are the road to nowhere.

You can perceive the positive at work. You can conceive it with other positive people at work. You can believe it and imagine the best for your work. You can even decide to pay attention to what God says is most important. However, if you just intend to act on it, you will never achieve a Faith Positive lifestyle in this negative world.

Ponder Your Faith Positive Work for a Moment   #FaithPos

Name one action you have intended to do as you read this book but have yet to do it.

Intention in Isolation

As you discover in the next chapter, intention can be a powerful catalyst when combined with attention and action in what we call The Achievement Prescription. However, like all catalysts, when isolated, intention is ineffective in producing a faith-reality reaction.

How do you know when your intention is just that— only an intention with no connection to God-initiated attention or action? What does it look like?

Fear.

As you pay attention to what God says is most important, know that fear lurks in the dark shadows of transition from attention to action, intent on derailing your Faith Positive lifestyle with doubt. Intention is the road to nowhere because without attention and action it morphs into fear. You dead-end and fear vanquishes your spiritual dreams.

Here are five traits of intention-generated fears to anticipate as you transition from attention to action.

1. Intention Fears Failure

For so many executives, entrepreneurs, and business owners, fear of failure paralyzes. It's why they analyze an opportunity until it's gone with no positive results. So many successful businessmen and women tell their stories of success, but virtually all of them have several chapters of failed previous attempts.

On New Year's Day, 1929, Georgia Tech played UCLA in the Rose Bowl. Roy Riggles recovered a fumble for UCLA, became confused, and ran sixty-five yards in the wrong direction. One of his teammates outran and tackled him just before he scored for the other team. When UCLA tried to punt, Tech blocked the kick and scored a safety.

That strange play came in the first half, and everyone watching the game was asking the same question: "What will Coach Price do with Roy Riggles in the second half?" Price said in the locker room, "Men, the same team that played the first half starts the second."

"Coach," Riggles said, "I can't do it. I couldn't face that crowd in the stadium to save my life."

Then Price said, "Roy, get up and go on back out there. The game is only half over."

Coach Price understood that failure is a play in the game, not the game itself. Faith Positive business professionals appreciate grace and understand that failure is an experience, not a person. It is a moment in which the expected result didn't appear for various reasons. Those mistakes receive the scrutiny, are corrected, and more attempts made.

As you increase faith with greater joy at work, make mistakes and then make new ones the next time. Learn and go back on the playing field of faith reality. Your faith increases as you do.

Ponder Your Faith Positive Work for a Moment   #FaithPos

What are you most afraid of failing at while you attempt to do it?

---

2. Intention Seeks Perfection Immediately

Intention fears failure and also seeks perfection immediately. You want to do something perfectly the first time.

With this fear in play, your business mistakes are fatal. The team knows it because you don't tolerate anything that smells like a mistake. Your customers know it because even when you make one, you won't admit it. You blame rather than take responsibility.

Mike coached a salesperson who knew the advantages of making face-to-face cold calls. He intended to follow his plan and make it all a reality.

But he never could put his plans into action. It was on his calendar each week for the entire year. He even practiced his opening statements and envisioned how these visits would look. However, each week on the appointed day, fear dominated his thoughts and paralyzed him. He was convinced he wouldn't do it perfectly so he didn't do it at all.

Did he have good intentions? The best! Did he plan to make the calls? Absolutely. Perfectionism took over until he finally gave up and removed the daily calls from his calendar. He resumed complaining about his lack of new business opportunities. Following his lead, his team joined in the negative atmosphere with talk of the poor economy and the dreadful competition.

Ponder Your Faith Positive Work for a Moment #FaithPos

What part of your work do you avoid because you fear you won't do it perfectly?

3. Intention Gives Up and Quits

Excuses for not achieving positive results at work arise from your fear of failure. You intend to do something but fear you will fail. Perfectionism is fear of failure on steroids.

The role of intention at its best is one of continuing the pursuit of your Faith Positive lifestyle even when the path zigs and zags. Even when you fail. Even when you fail the second time. Perseverance is the key. When isolated from attention to what God says is important and action God ordains, intention gives up and quits.

Walter Johnson was a legendary baseball pitcher, striking out batters at will. A rookie faced Johnson for the first time and, before he knew what happened, had two strikes called. He just shook his head and walked away from the batter's box.

The umpire took off his mask and called after the rookie, "Son, where are you going? That was just strike two."

"You keep the third strike," the rookie said. "I've seen enough."

It happens. You fear you simply won't make it and assume you know the outcome. You see enough at work and want to walk away and say to everyone involved, "You keep it," allowing the negative world to win.

There is something to be said for staying in the batter's box, even when you think you'll strike out. When you walk away, you learn nothing except how to quit. When you persevere, you learn something about yourself, about the situation, and what it takes to achieve positive results at work.

Ponder Your Faith Positive Work for a Moment   #FaithPos

When are you more likely to quit, under what circumstances?

---

4. Intention Underestimates the Power of One

Intention is the road to nowhere, to walking away when it is divorced from attention and action. Alone it underestimates the power you have as one person who perceives, conceives, and believes in a faith reality despite the negative world.

Is that a real challenge for you to believe—that you as one person can join Christ at work in transforming the negative world?

"Dr. Joey and Mike, you don't know where I work."

Do you ever wonder if what you do through your work matters?

"Guys, you don't know what I do."

Do you ever ask yourself if your work actions—the actions of one person in a company—make a difference?

We both travel through airports regularly. Each time we do, we stand in line with hundreds of others waiting to go through the preflight baggage check and screening. We take off our shoes and hope we wore our good socks.

Why do we take off our shoes? Because one young man attempted to detonate a shoe bomb in midair of one flight. One young man radically transformed the way the U.S. population flies.

Think of a more positive example from your own faith

journey. Who is the one person who introduced you to Christ? The one who mentored you in the faith? The one who discipled you?

Intention, denied God's chosen attention and ordained actions, breaks down into the fear that what you do has no effect on others. Pay attention to God's priorities and act according to The Plan and watch as your positive influence multiplies exponentially.

Ponder Your Faith Positive Work for a Moment   #FaithPos

What have you perceived, conceived, and believed you could achieve, and refused to pursue because you are "just one person"?

---

5. Intention Rushes to Results

Are you beginning to understand now why intention alone is the road to nowhere? What you meant to do at work to create more joy, but did not actually do, prevents you from achieving positive results. It fears failure, which shuts your action down, causing you to seek perfection immediately and give up and quit. It underestimates the power that you as one person have to transform the lives of your customers by solving their problems, spiritual and otherwise.

Occasionally intention does draw a bead on the bull's-eye of active results, but because it is divorced from attention, whatever action it prompts impatiently rushes to results. Your attention dissipates. You lack sufficient information to inform your actions.

Dr. Joey enjoys growing roses and was admiring his rosebushes one day. A few days later he noticed that almost all the blooms had faded and that even though there were plenty of buds, there just weren't any open flowers.

I wish these rosebuds would hurry up and open, or, at

least part of them. I wish there was something I could to do to speed them up, he thought.

Then it occurred to him that there is no way to unfold a rosebud more quickly without destroying it. Sure, he can water it regularly and feed it often, but he simply destroys a rosebud when attempting to open it with his hands. The rosebush is damaged when rushed.

Separated from God-focused attention and action, intention rushes you through your work at times. You damage your spiritual growth when you rush it.

Ponder Your Faith Positive Work for a Moment   #FaithPos

What aspect of your work are you most impatient with?

Why?

As you perceive, conceive, and believe during s u c h times of danger and opportunity, you begin to achieve dynamic results of growth that facilitate the display of your faith's best traits. Your core values, priorities, and unique contributions that separate you from the competition shine clearly into your relationships. As you avoid rushing through negative economic conditions, the challenges of each moment present themselves as alive and vibrant.

You do more than survive. You thrive.

And yet when these fears assault your faith, when the worry steals your joy, when the Eeyore Vampires suck the love from your relationships, it becomes extremely challenging to achieve your spiritual dreams. You look for a place to hide, a refuge.

King David knew this need for shelter from fear. In Psalm 91 he declares that God is his refuge that he trusts and feels safe from fear. Why?

"He rescues you from hidden traps, shields you from deadly hazards. His huge outstretched arms protect you. . . . *Fear nothing. . . .* He ordered his angels to guard you wherever you go. If you stumble, they'll catch you; their job is to keep you from falling" (Ps. 91:3–5, 11–12; emphasis added).

David confessed that fear is an opportunity for intimacy with God that increases your faith with greater joy at work so you love God and others more. Fear is your chance to trust God to rescue you from failed business attempts, to send angels to catch you when perfection eludes you, to shield you from the temptation to give up and quit, to wrap cosmic-sized arms around you when you underestimate your power, and to guard you when you feel like rushing to results.

Even David, a king after God's own heart, knew fear. You will know fear if you haven't already. Embrace the fear. Let it be your signal that your intentions are divorced from God-focused attention and God-driven action. Use the fear to push you to a vibrant, increasing faith with greater joy at work.

Think of fear and your Faith Positive lifestyle in this way. The Great Barrier Reef stretches some eighteen hundred miles from New Guinea to Australia. The lagoon side of the reef looks pale and lifeless, while the ocean side is vibrant and colorful. Why?

The coral on the lagoon side is in still water with no challenge for its survival. It dies early. The coral on the ocean side is constantly being tested by wind, waves, and storms—surges of power. It fights for survival every day of its life. It changes and adapts as it is challenged and tested. It grows healthier and stronger every day.

As you learn to increase faith with greater joy at work in this negative world, you are like that coral. Your work comes alive and grows when challenged and tested by economic storms. The untested aspects intend to grow but, unchallenged, atrophy. The challenged side confronts adversity daily, and therein is its success. That which could be seen as negative becomes the opportunity for proving your new faith reality.

Here is the key to understanding the true power of

intention: left alone, unchallenged, your intention to increase faith with greater joy at work is the road to nowhere. Fear is your only outcome. Partnering with God-focused attention and God-driven action, intention is a powerful catalyst that, like the ocean, stimulates a positive spiritual vitality that redefines your reality and achieves your dreams.

Ponder Your Faith Positive Work for a Moment   #FaithPos

Name one challenge you are experiencing right now in your work that, like the ocean, can be a source of stimulation and vitality for you.

Grab and *Go*

As you develop a Faith Positive lifestyle at work, remember, intention is the road to nowhere and:

1. Failure is a play in the game, not the game itself.

2. Perfection is the enemy of making face-to-face calls or anything else you do at work.

3. Stay in the batter's box and swing at all the opportunities thrown in your strike zone.

4. You have the power as one person, with Christ, in one organization to transform the lives of others.

5. Separated from God-focused attention and action, intention rushes you through your work at times. You damage your spiritual growth when you rush it.

CHAPTER 12

The Achievement Prescription

"I can do all things through Christ who strengthens me."
—Philippians 4:13, NKJV

Attention (perceive and conceive) plus intention (believe) is an excellent beginning to achieving positive results in your work, to bringing to life what you perceive as positive, conceive with other positive people, and believe will happen as you imagine the best. However, one ingredient in your prescription for achieving your spiritual dreams is still missing. That missing element is action.

Action brings achievement. Jesus put it this way:

"Ask and you'll receive."

"Knock and it'll open."

"Seek and you'll find it" (see Matt. 7:7–8).

Each affirmation begins with an active verb. You have to do something to get the positive results you desire.

What if Jesus had said:

"Sit there with your mouth closed, expect people to read your mind, and you'll receive."

"Just stand there, staring at the door, and it'll open for you."

"Relax in your favorite recliner and see what shows up on your front porch."

Sure you may be giving some attention to the situation, and you intend to do something about it. However, unless you act—create some movement, get some traction—you fail to redefine your reality into God's faith reality and fulfill the spiritual dreams of your Faith Positive lifestyle.

Action is the critical ingredient to physically achieving your Faith Positive lifestyle. You pay attention to the positive thoughts (perceive) and positive people (conceive) God shows you are most important. Your intentions emerge from your emotional engagement with faith reality (believe). Action applied to your attention and intention propels you to achieve your spiritual dreams.

Think of it as The Achievement Prescription:

Attention + Intention + ACTION = Achievement of the Faith Positive Lifestyle

How Do You Act Best?

Perhaps you're wondering, "How do I strategically act to redefine reality into God's faith reality and achieve my spiritual dreams in such a negative world?"

In our coaching practices we discovered two primary action traits of Faith Positive business professionals. They are:

1. Listen to constant feedback.
2. Act Faith Positive regardless.

1. Listen to Constant Feedback

Think of constant feedback as the results of your action. When you avoid perceiving only familiar thoughts, you march off your mental map into what is uncharted territory. When you compare and compete rarely, you cease using Eeyore Vampires as a reference point and instead conceive positively with others, listening carefully. When you move away from your bent to ego, you begin to imagine the best possible business outcomes by living into your birthright to believe. As you act on the positive results you perceive, conceive, and believe, you discover that some of your actions produce dramatic results in the bottom line. You also discover some ways of doing business that don't work so well. You quickly learn to do more of the former and less of the latter.

Constant feedback evaluates your actions in producing positive results. It serves you as a course correction. Think of constant feedback as your Faith Positive GPS.

We both have a GPS in our vehicles. It directs us where and when to turn. When we take a turn the GPS does not recommend, it then recalculates and advises us accordingly. "Miles" (the Australian male voice on Dr. Joey's wife's GPS) says something like, "Recalculating" or "Please make a U-turn when possible" or gives her the best street to turn on to get back on route. So far "Miles" has yet to call her an idiot or a fool or ask her, "What were you thinking?" or "Are you asleep or stupid?" He simply recalculates and redirects her.

The negative world wants you to call yourself an idiot or a fool or to ask yourself, "What was I thinking? Oh, wait, I wasn't," or "Are you asleep or stupid?" when your efforts produce less positive results and your faith decreases, your joy at work slips away, and your love for God and others is lost.

Instead of placing a negative value judgment on you or your business driving abilities, simply receive the constant feedback of those actions that are more effective than others and pursue them. Do those actions more often in your day-to-day business. Facilitate the results as just that—results—and feed them back into how you perceive, conceive, and believe for future actions. Just as "Miles" says, "Recalculate" and do what works best to get you back on the preferred path of a positive faith reality despite the negative world.

Remember how, when at your best, you imagine what God helps you believe in by sending the Spirit to work within you deeply and gently? The Spirit is another source of constant feedback you listen to as you recalculate your way to positive success. At this intersection of business feedback—customers, teammates, and vendors—and spiritual feedback you achieve your spiritual dreams.

Think of this deep, gentle Spirit as your internal GPS, God's Positive Spirit, nudging you in the best direction to increase faith with greater joy at work so you love God and others more. Your role is to continue traveling, not in time—past and future—but in the present moment, giving your entire attention to what God is doing in and through you to give you an abundant, Faith Positive life.

Act on what you hear as you listen to the recalculating feedback of your business GPS and your internal GPS (God's Positive Spirit). Your perseverance gathers more fruit for everyone served by your work. Your Faith Positive lifestyle grows dramatically.

Ponder Your Faith Positive Work for a Moment #FaithPos

When did you "make a mistake," learn from it, and course correct your work to a positive outcome?

Name a recent "mistake" at work and perceive how you can course correct to a positive outcome.

2. Act Faith Positive Regardless

At times you don't recalculate. You allow negativity to creep into your perceiving. You invite Eeyore Vampires into the circle of people with whom you conceive. You let the "can't-do-its" leap into what you believe. You compare and compete and give in to the temptation to stop acting, to slip into "paralysis by analysis" mode.

At this intersection you must increase your faith, moving in God's faith reality toward positive results no matter what. You say to yourself, "I can do all things through Christ who strengthens me" (Phil. 4:13, NKJV).

Why are Paul's words important here to your increasing faith, greater joy, and more love?

First, "I can do." Eeyore Vampires circle your action like vultures searching for dying efforts. They whisper, "It'll never work," sucking your "can-do" beliefs.

By repeating this verse, you remind yourself, "Yes, I can do." You remember to focus on the positive, to collaborate with positive people, to imagine your work at its best, and to immerse yourself in the redefined faith reality.

Second, "all things." There are no exceptions. *All* means "everything." Sure, challenges that would paralyze your actions seem personal and unique to you. They aren't. Paul knew them all and more firsthand. So do we, all our clients, and everyone else who has ever tried to achieve anything that's God sized. Even Jesus confronted this reality. Yes, you can do all things. How?

Third, "through Christ who strengthens me." Yes, you are still in a carpool. Christ is driving. You are riding. And "oh the places you will go!" (Dr. Seuss). Remember the GPS in your business and the GPS (God's Positive Spirit) within you? Through Christ's strength you recalculate your action to positive success. Your weakness is countered by Christ's strength.

Since you can do all things through Christ who strengthens you, you persevere. You take action and achieve a Faith Positive lifestyle. The longer we coach executives, entrepreneurs, and business owners, and the more we study the spiritual traits of positively successful business professionals, the more convinced we are of the importance of persevering.

For instance, Abraham Lincoln went bankrupt as a business owner and lost more political elections than he won on his way to the White House and salvaging our war-torn nation. On his way to becoming what is perhaps the highest paid comedian in the world, Jerry Seinfeld forgot all his jokes the first time he did stand-up comedy, got fired from a TV show because he could not act, and had his show cancelled. Michael Jordan was cut from the basketball team at Laney High School in Wilmington, North Carolina, in his freshman year along the way to becoming what many consider the best basketball player in modern history. In creating the lightbulb, Thomas Edison survived a laboratory fire that destroyed all his notes with thousands of ways not to make a lightbulb. The country music group Alabama was dubbed an "overnight success" in the late 1970s, and yet they had been playing and touring for many years, twelve years at The Bowery in Myrtle Beach, South Carolina. John Grisham sold copies of his first book out of the trunk of his car in Charlottesville, Virginia, and other places he could drive between court cases before achieving the title of "best-selling author."

Vincent Van Gogh created eight hundred paintings but sold only one in his lifetime. He died at thirty-seven, and the first one-man exhibit of his works occurred after his death. Tom Landry, Chuck Noll, and Bill Walsh accounted for nine of the fifteen Super Bowl victories from 1974 to 1989. They also had the worst records of first-season head coaches in NFL history. Test pilot Chuck Yeager said, "I have learned to back up, but I never give up."

You can back up but not give up like Chuck Yeager and all these other persons who achieved positive results. If you truly want to increase faith with greater joy at work so you love God and others more, you perceive, conceive, and believe in the positive factors of your work, and then you redefine your reality to a faith reality and achieve your spiritual dreams. You transform the impossible into the possible by listening to constant feedback and persevering to act Faith Positive regardless.

> **Ponder Your Faith Positive Work for a Moment** #FaithPos
>
> Who is someone you know who was tempted to give up,
> did not, and achieved positive results? Tell yourself that
> person's story right now.

Achieving Faith Positive Results

The positive results you achieve are astoundingly simple and profound at times.

Dr. Joey took his lunch hour one day to visit a friend with cancer in the hospital. He walked in just as the nurse appeared in the doorway and said, "I'm sorry, we don't have any" to the patient.

Dr. Joey's friend said: "I'll bet you're wondering what I asked for. Toothpicks. I asked if they had any toothpicks. I just love my toothpicks after I eat."

As he walked down the hall after their visit, Dr. Joey thought, *There she is, dying from cancer, and all she wants is a toothpick.* As he rode down the elevator, his internal GPS pointed out a direction: "Go get her a box of toothpicks. It's such a little thing."

So Dr. Joey went to the grocery store, bought a box of toothpicks, and returned to the hospital, where she was eating, and said, "I have just what you'll want after your meal" and handed her the toothpicks. Her look of surprise and laughter are his last memories of her.

> **Ponder Your Faith Positive Work for a Moment** #FaithPos
>
> What is "one little thing" you can do for someone you
> work with that will become large to him or her?

Sometimes it's the little things in life that become large when you achieve positive results.

As you act on your spiritual intentions to which you have

given your attention, the positive results you perceived, conceived, and believed could happen actually do. Your reality redefines and, working in a faith reality, you fulfill your spiritual dreams. You positively succeed even in a negative world.

You become so positively successful that you wonder, "What do I do next?"

In that moment you discover that while you have acted on the Faith Positive core practices to perceive, conceive, believe, and achieve increasing faith with greater joy at work so you love God and others more, you have in reality received it. Out of gratitude you now desire above and beyond anything else to say thank you and to squeeze yourself dry as you serve others and live out of the fifth core practice of your Faith Positive lifestyle.

Grab and *Go*

Take The Achievement Prescription.

1. Attention + Intention + ACTION = Achievement of the Faith Positive Lifestyle.

2. Ask to receive. Knock to open. Seek to find.

3. Follow your faith-reality GPS (God's Positive Spirit) and recalculate to positive success.

4. I can do. All things. Through Christ.

5. Persevere like Abraham Lincoln, Jerry Seinfeld, Michael Jordan, Thomas Edison, Alabama, John Grisham, Vincent Van Gogh, Tom Landry, Chuck Noll, Bill Walsh, and Chuck Yeager.

receive the positive in faith at work

Receive the Positive in Faith at Work

"For God so loved the world that He gave."

—John 3:16, NKJV

When Dr. Joey's wife was pregnant with their first child, she really wanted a certain kind of baby crib, the Jenny Lind crib. Frankly, he didn't have enough money to buy it but wanted to purchase it because it meant that much to her.

So he remembered his shotgun. He had not hunted with it for years; yet it was still special to him. Santa Claus brought it to him when he was thirteen. It was a kind of rite-of-passage gift on his way to becoming a man. Think of it as a "redneck Bar Mitzvah" gift.

It was his "dream gun"—a Remington 870 Wingmaster pump action, 12 gauge with a 28-inch modified choke barrel and walnut stock. Not that he was attached to the gun or anything like that.

Dr. Joey decided that the crib was coming and the gun was going. He would sell the shotgun and buy the baby crib. On his way to the gun shop to sell it, he stopped by to visit a friend, James, who said he wanted it. So Dr. Joey sold the shotgun to him and bought the crib, presenting it to his wife as a surprise baby gift. She loved it!

About fourteen years later, on his fortieth birthday, Dr. Joey's wife threw a huge birthday party for him. She had about 250 of his closest friends over for a meal and party.

After everyone left, she escorted him into their home and said: "There's one more thing. Close your eyes and hold out your hands, and I will give you a big surprise."

Dr. Joey did, and she said: "OK, open your eyes! Here's your birthday present," and she handed him the Remington Wingmaster 12-gauge shotgun he had sold to buy the Jenny Lind baby crib.

"Where did you get it?" he said.

"From James," she said. "I called him and told him that you were turning forty and asked him if I could buy your gun back. And Joey," she said, "he wouldn't let me pay him. He gave it to me as your present."

Ponder Your Faith Positive Work for a Moment #FaithPos

Remember when someone gave you a surprise gift of great sentimental value. What was that experience like for you?

When you perceive, conceive, believe, and achieve a Faith Positive lifestyle and give it away to others, you receive back more of the same faith reality.

Knowing how to perceive a Faith Positive lifestyle in this negative world, focusing on the positive while avoiding just the "familiar," and then placing the positive filter on your thoughts is the first core practice. It is the mental dynamic of increasing faith with greater joy at work so you love God and others more.

The second core practice is to attract your team, customers, and suppliers based on your core values, priorities, and unique contribution you make. Together you conceive how to cooperate and surround yourself with these positive people who collaborate. Conceive is the social dynamic of enjoying a Faith Positive lifestyle.

The third core practice is to redefine your reality of work into God's faith reality and believe you can be Faith Positive even in a negative world, avoid your bent to ego, and imagine your success at its best. Believe is the emotional dynamic of a Faith Positive lifestyle.

The fourth core practice—the physical dynamic—describes how you achieve a Faith Positive lifestyle even in a negative world by acting on your attention and intention. You pay attention to what's important to God, align your intention by vanquishing fear, and act on achieving the impossible.

This fifth and final core practice is about the unique rewards and delightful experiences you have as you work Faith Positive and share what you've received. Think about it as your ministry through work. Receive describes the ethical dynamic of how you increase faith with greater at work so you love God and others more.

CHAPTER 13

Say "Thank You"

"Give thanks to God."

—Psalm 136:1, authors' translation

D r. Ivan Misner, the founder of BNI (Business Network International), created this franchised referral network of business people on the philosophy of "Givers Gain.®" For Dr. Misner, when you refer business to other members in your chapter, you literally gain more business because you give. Our faith reality understands it as God rooted the universe in the eternal principle that when you give to others, you receive.

Think about your own work for a moment. Have you ever said, "I went to help Harry out, and he helped me more"? Or, "I told Suzie about John and how he's a great guy to buy a car from, and six people showed up in my store the other day saying John sent them"?

It happens. Givers Gain.®

As you have become Faith Positive and work into your faith reality these five core practices to perceive, conceive, believe, and achieve positive results in this negative world, you discover something. You have started to receive positive results. Your faith is increasing. You're finding greater joy at work. You love God and others more.

Everything you have done has been guided by your internal GPS—God's Positive Spirit. This book has guided you. We were guided by the same Spirit in writing this book.

You learned how your mind works best and used it accordingly. Yet did you create your brain?

You discovered how relationships are best lived into and started doing that. Yet did you seek out all those positive people?

You realized that you were born to believe and could actually imagine your work at its best. And yet did you give birth to yourself?

You recognized that as you paid more attention to your perceiving, conceiving, and believing, and then acted, the positive results started showing up on the faces of your satisfied customers, in the handwritten notes your vendor started sending, and in the looks of gratitude your teammates started giving you.

You work these important first four practices to the best of your ability, and yet it all comes down to the simple recognition that as your reality redefines and your spiritual dreams are fulfilled, you receive your Faith Positive lifestyle.

Have you ever said, "What goes around, comes around?"

What did you mean by that?

Givers Gain.®

Have you ever said, "You reap what you sow" (see Gal. 6:7)?

What does that mean to you?

In the faith reality you receive your Faith Positive lifestyle.

These two statements describe what you have done in the previous four core practices. So what else can you say but "Thank you!" as you receive a Faith Positive lifestyle?

Psychologists have discovered that God created you to say and hear "Thank you!" and respond with happiness. Martin Seligman (*Authentic Happiness)* and Shawn Achor *(The Happiness Advantage)* and others found that those receiving a thank-you were much more likely to offer more help to the one offering the thanks than to those who didn't show their gratitude. Also, those receiving thank-yous were more likely to help others in addition to helping the person offering the thank-you.

Do You Say "Thank You" to Your Customers?

When you realize you receive your Faith Positive lifestyle, your attitude becomes one of gratitude. You want to say "Thank you!" to someone. Have you thought about starting with your customers?

One of our favorite books is Tim Sanders' *Love Is the Killer App: How to Win Business and Influence Friends* (www.TimSanders.com). He tells the story of his friend Mike, who was president of Pizza Hut. Every Friday during his lunch hour, Mike called his MVCs—Most Valuable Customers—to say, "Thank you for your business."

One Friday, Mike called a customer in a poor neighborhood in south Dallas who ordered more than a dozen large pizzas a month for a year. "From the bottom of my heart," he told her, "I want to thank you for your business." Then he asked the mother, "Tell me why you order our pizza. What's your story?"

The mother told Mike her story of being a divorced mother of five children, three to eleven in age, and how she worked three jobs to support them. She didn't want her kids to see their mom accepting public assistance so she worked virtually nonstop. She let the eldest order pizza as a kind of reward because "my kids really love pizza."

Mike was so moved by her story that he said, "Ma'am, I want to thank you for something entirely different from being a good customer. I want to thank you for being a good mother."

Mike called to give and gained again.

> ## Ponder Your Faith Positive Work for a Moment #FaithPos
>
> How do you say "Thank you!" to your customers or
> clients? When was the last time you did so? Write down
> three ways you say "Thank you!" to them.

Do You Say "Thank You!" to Your Teammates?

A dear friend of Dr. Joey's served as the general manager of a rapidly growing manufacturing company. One day over lunch, the two discussed how they say "Thank you!" to employees rather than just assuming they exchange money for time and ability.

They talked about the gift of presence that responds in more than the obvious, expected events of life. Dr. Joey's friend told the story of how an employee was on the brink of financial disaster due to unforeseen life events. She had come to the operations manager about the situation and explained she may not be at her best productivity because of the stress. The ops manager shared the predicament with Dr. Joey's friend, who asked, "How much does she need?"

The OM said something about her inability to pay it back, but the GM simply said again, "How much does she need?"

Hearing the amount, Dr. Joey's friend said, "Give it to her, and tell her to pay it back as she can."

She paid it back as she could, a little at a time, and became one of the most productive employees in the company. She constantly bragged on her workplace and how much management cares for its employees, unlike other companies. By doing so, she helped the company attract top talent, which increased productivity and profits even more.

Dr. Joey's friend gave and gained more. He worked out of a faith reality and ministered through the business.

> ## Ponder Your Faith Positive Work for a Moment #FaithPos
>
> How do you say "Thank you!" to your teammates? When was the last time you did so? Write down three ways you say "Thank you!" to them.

King David said it best, over and over again in Psalm 136: "Give thanks to God!" (authors' translation).

Here's one way for you to give thanks to customers and teammates alike, just as David did to God—write it down. In this pixelated world of e-mails and texts, Facebook and Twitter, the simple and quick act of writing a handwritten expression of gratitude goes a long way with many of your customers and teammates. There's something special today about a handwritten note, especially to those who miss it as a thing of the past.

Others would prefer a tweet, text, or e-mail of gratitude. Find out how others like their thank-you, and share it with them their way. For those who are more touched by a handwritten note, keep a stack of cards and envelopes with you to write on the go. It takes about three minutes per card. For those who would rather read it on their phone or tablet, send your gratitude to them digitally.

You create "Givers Gain"® business when you take pen or mobile device in hand and write, "Thank you!" to your customers. Just say something like, "I know you could do business with others, but you chose us. Thank you! We treasure our relationship."

You create greater joy at work when you write, tweet, e-mail, or text thank-you notes to your teammates. Just say, "I really appreciate you (name the specific act) the other day for me. It really made a big difference in my day! Thank you so much!" You create a "Givers Gain"® work environment as you do.

Can you imagine how much better our world will be when more and more of us start to say "Thank you!" from our faith reality and fulfilled spiritual dreams?

Ponder Your Faith Positive Work for a Moment   #FaithPos

Who is one person you know who could use a copy of this book? One person you could buy and give a copy of this book to create a more positive world in which "Thank you!" is heard more often?

Grab and Go

Remember these as you say "Thank you!"

1. Write, tweet, and e-mail a personal thank-you to someone at least once a week. Be specific with your gratitude.

2. Givers Gain® (Dr. Ivan Misner, BNI)

3. "What goes around comes around."

4. "You reap what you sow."

5. Ultimately, you receive your Faith Positive lifestyle.

CHAPTER 14

Squeeze Yourself Dry

"You must now wash each other's feet."

—John 13:13

I f you put a sponge under running water, within a few minutes it is saturated. It can hold no more water.

But what if you left the sponge under the running water for five more minutes? Would it hold any more?

Perhaps if you left the sponge under the running water for a whole day it would hold more?

What would you have to do for the sponge to hold more water?

Squeeze it out. Only when you squeeze the sponge will it hold more water.

As you enjoy a Faith Positive lifestyle of increasing faith with greater joy at work so you love God and others more, you are like a sponge. You can only soak up more as you squeeze your life and give away the positive you have received to someone else. As you give away the positive results, you create room within yourself and your work for achieving more of your spiritual dreams.

Ponder Your Faith Positive Work for a Moment   #FaithPos

Recall the last time you squeezed yourself and shared
your positive results. Maybe you gave some surplus
clothes to a clothes closet ministry. Or chaired a cancer
fund-raiser. Or gave frequent flier miles to a young couple
for their honeymoon. Or some other squeezing occasion ...
what did you do?

Think about It This Way

If your hands are full, how can someone hand you
something?

What if your hands are full, and someone wants to
hand you something, and you want that something they
are handing you more than what you are holding? What
will you do?

Put down what you're holding. Empty your hands to
receive.

If you hang on to your most recent positive achievement
so long that you begin to claim credit for it, your hands
are full and you can't receive anything but the accolades
and applause that accompany the experience. You deny
yourself the next great positive experience.

There is a penalty in college football for "bringing too
much attention to oneself" after scoring. This rule intends
to develop good sportsmanship among these young men in
stark contrast to the NFL players they emulate who begin
their bent-to-ego antics when in the act of scoring and
continue them after the play to gain more celebrity status
and a larger contract.

As in football, so it is as you work in the faith reality
God designs. Faith Positive is a team sport.

Ponder Your Faith Positive Work for a Moment #FaithPos

Remember an occasion at work when you could have been penalized for "bringing too much attention to yourself." What choices did you make that drove you to do that?

Who Is Squeezing Whom?

Jesus told a story about a client who requested a meeting with his banker and the conversation went something like this:

As you know, I have always paid on time when you have lent me money. I've always been conscientious about making my payments and on time. However, currently I find myself in a bit of a jam. The people who owe me money are not paying at all instead of just a little late. I'm here today to request that you restructure my debt, extending the period longer, and giving me a grace period of thirty extra days to come up with a payment.

The banker agreed to the terms, had the contract drawn up, and both lender and borrower were satisfied.

As the client left the bank, relieved to have the new terms in hand, he saw someone walking on the other side of the street who owed him money.

"Hey!" he yelled loudly enough for everyone on Main Street to hear. "Come here. You owe me money!"

Running across the street while dodging traffic, he grabbed the guy's arm and said, "Where's my money? You think you can just take my money and not pay it back? That's a crime, my friend."

He forced the man into a nearby magistrate's office, filed a complaint, and had the man thrown into jail.

Meanwhile, the banker heard some commotion on Main Street from his third-floor corner office and lifted the window to see what was happening. He watched in horror as the client that had just been forgiven his previous terms of payment accosted another man, drug him into the magistrate's office, and emerged alone. The banker knew the magistrate so he called to inquire about the incident. Much to his chagrin, he discovered that the client had the man imprisoned.

The banker then said to the magistrate, "Well, I have a complaint of my own to file." He rescinded the extension of terms for the client and had the magistrate swear out a warrant for his arrest. Before the day was over, the client was in the jail cell next to the man he had imprisoned.

What goes around, comes around.

You reap what you sow.

Ponder Your Faith Positive Work for a Moment #FaithPos

Recall a life experience when you failed to pass on the positive results you received. What was the outcome for you? for others?

God increases your faith with greater joy at work so you love Him and others in proportion to what you do with what you receive. Think of your work as a conduit for blessings to flow through you and to others. The faith. The joy. The love. And yes, the money.

Your Faith Positive lifestyle works like the sponge under running water. You squeeze yourself dry to receive more.

As your faith increases, you trust God more. You give more and receive more which builds a more intimate, credible relationship with your Creator. The kind Jesus enjoyed.

When he gathered with his best friends for a last meal before his crucifixion and resurrection, Jesus humbled himself and washed their feet. He squeezed himself of any ego needs and bathed their smelly, callused feet.

That's the last place you would expect the One who was

present when the universe was created, the divine Son of God, the Christ who came down from heaven to be found. As a common servant, stooping down, on his hands and knees, to wash his best friends' nasty feet.

Peter had trouble getting his head wrapped around this paradox. It challenged his understanding of what it means to be God, to be powerful, to be "large and in charge." He pushed back against Jesus' example, primarily because he knew what it meant—if Jesus did it, he would have to squeeze himself dry also. He had fought off James's and John's mother's appeal for her sons to sit on the right and left hands of Jesus when he came into power, leaving no room near the throne. How was he to fend off this redefinition of the abundant life?

As Peter protested this paradigm of power-gifting, Jesus said to him, "My concern . . . is holiness, not hygiene." (John 13:11). He went on to tell them, "If I, the Master and Teacher, washed your feet, you must now wash each other's feet. I've laid down a pattern for you. What I've done, you do. . . . If you understand what I'm telling you, act like it—*and live a blessed life* (13:14–15, 17; emphasis added).

Live a blessed life by squeezing yourself dry.

What goes around, comes around.

You reap what you sow.

Give to receive.

Here's another way to think about it. Let's say we lend you a million dollars. You agree to start making interest-free payments of $10,000 by the middle of each month until your loan is satisfied.

On the first of each month, we send you a check for $10,000 for you to use to make your monthly payment.

Get the picture now?

The greatest challenge you have in the negative world is squeezing yourself dry and trusting that as you squeeze, you will receive more.

Trust God who created an abundant universe, an infinite

source of resources waiting to be yours as you become Faith Positive.

> ## Ponder Your Faith Positive Work for a Moment   #FaithPos
>
> Recall a particularly important time in your work when someone squeezed themselves dry to help you. What did that experience do for you? For you work? How can you squeeze yourself dry for another person in similar fashion?

Anticipate the Unexpected

Peter misunderstood Jesus at first. Then he learned what Jesus meant—as you squeeze yourself and your work dry, you get some unexpected, pleasant outcomes in your new faith reality.

Mike sat with his neighbor as they did many evenings after work. His friend shared that he had rehired a young woman to help him in his business. Mike questioned that decision as this employee had gotten into some trouble and had proven before to be a difficult employee.

The neighbor pulled his chair a little closer to Mike's, looked him in the eye, and said, "We are self-employed businessmen. We can help persons who have made mistakes and give them another chance."

He went on to describe the many blessings God had given both of them, and the greatest blessing was their ability to help others. He gave Mike a lot to think about that evening.

The next day a former employee of Mike's called asking for help finding work. She didn't ask to come to work for him, but Mike remembered the conversation from the night before. While on the phone, he offered her a position to begin work immediately. He was considering adding someone to help him with the "stuff" that comes with owning a business. She filled the role with such success that it gave him more time to visit with customers and spend with his family. Mike's neighbor taught him the law of squeezing yourself dry so God can fill you up again.

Sometimes you squeeze yourself and your work dry, and you get an unexpected, pleasant surprise. Something happens you didn't see coming. You give and you receive beyond your expectations. You pass on positive success and receive more as you increase faith with greater joy at work so you love God and others more.

Be prepared for anything God wants you to receive in your new faith reality.

Grab and Go

As you squeeze yourself dry, remember:

1. Squeeze a sponge so it will hold more water. Squeeze your Faith Positive work so it holds more positive results.

2. Empty your hands to receive. Empty your work, also, and make room for more.

3. There is a penalty in college football for "bringing too much attention to oneself" after scoring. Share the glory when you score.

4. God increases your faith, joy, and love in proportion to what you do with what you receive.

5. Wash others' feet.

CHAPTER 15

Serve Others

"Forget yourselves long enough to lend a helping hand."

—Philippians 2:4

One spring Dr. Joey hung a bird feeder in an oak tree just outside an office window. He liked watching cardinals so he Googled them and discovered the kind of bird feed they prefer—sunflower seeds—and put lots of them in the feeder. About a dozen different families of cardinals came to the feeder. The key, he discovered, was offering them what they preferred.

Dr. Joey gave the cardinals what they wanted and received he wanted. When you give, you receive. God wove this universal principle into the fabric of everyday life:

- Givers gain.
- What goes around, comes around.
- You reap what you sow.

As Paul wrote to the Philippians, "Put yourself aside, and help others get ahead. Don't be obsessed with getting your own advantage. Forget yourselves long enough to lend a helping hand" (2:3–4).

Have an Attitude of Gratitude

For Paul the key to tapping into the power of this universal principle of "give and receive" is a motivation of thanksgiving, primarily for Jesus Christ's "selfless, obedient life and . . . death" (Phil. 2:8). To have an attitude of gratitude.

Your faith is increasing. Your joy at work is greater. You love God and others more.

Your spiritual dreams are fulfilling in the new faith reality. You are learning the vast riches—time, money, relationships—of what it means to be Faith Positive. You respond to all of these blessings with an attitude of gratitude, which prompts you to serve others. You give thanks for what you received by offering others what they prefer.

Ponder Your Faith Positive Work for a Moment   #FaithPos

Consider how you can serve others through the unique contribution provided by your work, as a part of your Faith Positive lifestyle so you can make a life, not just a living.

The ways in which you can serve others   a r e both uniquely yours and universally human. Your unique contribution to the world through your business is a ministry offering of service to meet the needs of others. It's at the corner of your contribution and the world's needs that the Faith Positive lifestyle does business.

For example, Dr. Joey was in a BNI chapter with a man who owns a dry-cleaning business. "What do you find most fulfilling about what you do?" Dr. Joey asked.

He talked about a family whose home burned. One of the only things salvaged was the little girl's teddy bear. Now this teddy bear was in pretty rough shape—covered with soot and stains, soaked from the fire hoses, and didn't smell good. The little girl absolutely loved this teddy bear, and it was all she had left after the fire.

The dry cleaner took on the mission of cleaning the teddy bear. He worked on the little bear's soot stains until they were gone. He cleaned and sanitized the bear so he smelled better. "That was one happy little girl when I was through," he said, "And that's why I love to do what I do. I get to make a difference."

This man serves others, meeting people with what they need. He lives a Faith Positive lifestyle in a negative world.

As your faith increases with greater joy at work so you love God and others more, you serve others, knowing that givers gain, that what goes around comes around, that you reap what you sow, primarily motivated by an attitude of gratitude.

You may be thinking, *Come on guys I can't clean teddy bears. I*... and you list what you do, unable to connect the dots between serving others and your list. That's OK. We understand. So did Jesus.

He said we all can serve some basic human needs. His list went something like this:

"I was hungry and you fed me,

I was thirsty and you gave me a drink,

I was homeless and you gave me a room,

I was shivering and you gave me clothes,

I was sick and you stopped to visit,

I was in prison and you came to see me" (Matt. 25:36, MSG).

So what about it? Can you take an hour or so off and cook?

Pour a cup of water?

Got an extra bedroom or hotel travel points to offer?

Some clothes in your closet you didn't wear last season?

A few minutes to stop by the hospital?

A Bible story to tell in a prison?

Jesus said, "Whenever you did one of these things to someone overlooked or ignored, that was me—you did it to me" (Matt. 25:40, MSG)

Ponder Your Faith Positive Work for a Moment #FaithPos

Whom can you serve right now? Think of someone you work with who could use a reason to be grateful.

What can you do for someone other than a person who has already served you?

Think of one of your customers who could use a reason to be grateful.

When will you do it?

As we serve one another out of the abundance of our work, the negative world becomes more positive. Like a rising tide, all the lifeboats around us are lifted up. Together, as human beings, we live out of our common hope to redefine into a faith reality and fulfill our collective spiritual dreams. We celebrate with you as you fulfill your spiritual dreams and you celebrate with us as our companies succeed. That which was impossible becomes possible. We increase our faith with greater joy at work, and together we love God and others more.

We discover our Faith Positive lifestyle as we serve others. Our reality redefines from "Finders keepers, losers weepers" to "The first shall be last, and the last shall be first."

Service motivated by an attitude of gratitude brings sustenance. God created the universe to support it—givers gain; what goes around, comes around; you reap what you sow.

We perceive, conceive, believe, and achieve positive results, which expands our positive thoughts, attracts more positive people, strengthens our beliefs, and creates more positive achievements. Together, serving one another, we become more Faith Positive oriented than any one of us alone. The world transforms from a negative place to a positive paradise like the one God intended from the beginning.

Husbands serve their wives by selling shotguns to purchase baby cribs. Wives serve their husbands by buying shotguns back. And friends serve husbands and wives by giving the shotguns back.

Our faith increases with greater joy at work so we love God and others more.

Grab and Go

Serve others as you remind yourself:

1. Sell your shotgun to buy the crib. Watch as the shotgun returns.

2. Just as with birds, serve others at work exactly what they want, not what you think they should have.

3. Serve everyone at work with an attitude of gratitude.

4. The faith reality transforms "Finders keepers, losers weepers" to "The first shall be last and the last shall be first."

5. Together, serving one another, our faith increases with greater joy at work so we love God and others more.

Celebrate and Sustain Your Faith Positive Lifestyle

"He who has begun a good work in you will complete it."
—Philippians1:6, NKJV

Congratulations! Thank you for reading this book to the end. Reading this far makes you more motivated to increase your faith with greater joy at work so you love God and others more. You are on a journey now as you work from the five core practices of a Faith Positive lifestyle.

You created some new neural pathways to perceive your Faith Positive lifestyle, discontent to dwell only in the Land of the Familiar ways you've worked. You chose to focus on the positive and filter out the negative world so you are "in the world" and "not of it."

You now conceive your positive thoughts with other positive people, enjoying collaborative relationships of cooperation with them. You have kicked a few Eeyore Vampires to the curb because it costs too much to do business with some people.

You claimed your birthright to believe that there is a

faith reality for your work in which you find it best to imagine what you and God can do together. You chose to bend toward the best rather than your ego, while you watch resources converge that exceed your imagination.

All of your efforts to perceive, conceive, and believe that you can be Faith Positive emerge in results you achieve. Your attention focuses on what is most important to God, and, coupled with your God-driven intentions that vanquish fear and God-directed actions, you redefine your reality and fulfill your spiritual dreams. The impossible is now possible.

Finally, you discovered that you are grateful for the many gifts you receive in your positively successful work. Your gratitude spills over from your heart as you squeeze yourself dry and serve others with an attitude of gratitude.

You increase your faith with greater joy at work and love God and others more. You are Faith Positive.

Here's a Word for the Journey

Let us offer you a word about the next leg of your work journey:

It's going to be difficult.

Continuing to grow your Faith Positive lifestyle is the new challenge. That takes more than reading this book.

Negativity will creep back in as you close this book. Slowly at first. Almost imperceptibly. But count on it—the negative world definitely will wedge back into your work.

You can continue to work Faith Positive once you put this book down, but it takes insightful, consistent equipping, encouraging, and edifying in this negative world.

So how do you do it?

We make it easy for you to continue growing your Faith Positive lifestyle.

You will:

- Discover more in-depth, biblical ways to increase your faith with greater joy at work to love God and others more with our online video coaching program, "7 Weeks to Faith Positive."

- Get equipped, encouraged, and edified in Scripture weekly with the Faith Positive Master Coaching Program.
- Learn with a Faith Positive coach monthly who helps personally design a spiritual growth plan for you.
- Gather with other Christian business professionals in your community or as a part of your church's small-group ministry.
- Participate in state, regional, and national conferences and workshops with others who want to grow more Faith Positive like you.
- Receive your certification as a Faith Positive coach from a divinity school and get credit toward a master's in Christian studies degree or on a noncredit basis.
- Enjoy other, to-be-imagined ways of equipping, encouraging, and edifying you in your pursuit of the Faith Positive lifestyle.

All the resources you want to increase your faith with greater joy at work so you love God and others more are available now.

Discover how simple it really is to celebrate and sustain your Faith Positive lifestyle daily.

Go to www.GetPositive.Today.

Or call 1.877.4DRJOEY.

Our God-sized mission is bigger than this book. Our mission is to coach so many businesspeople to redefine work into a faith reality and fulfill their spiritual dreams that the negative world is transformed into the positive paradise God intended at its genesis. Our mission is to join Christ in redeeming the world—in the world and not of it. Our mission is to prompt you to work with the Spirit who is deeply and gently with you.

With God, it's all possible.

By reading this book, you joined this mission. We invite you to continue your Faith Positive journey.

Many of us are already on the road to positive success together. There is room for you and your friends to come along.

Let's transform this negative world so that all the business professionals we know become Christians and enjoy a Faith Positive lifestyle.

AFTERWORD
Mark Whitacre, Ph.D.
The Informant

When you go to work today, imagine having a tape recorder attached to your chest, a second one in your briefcase and a third one in a special notebook, knowing that you will be secretly taping your supervisors, coworkers, and in some cases, your friends. Now imagine doing that every day for three years.

That is exactly what I did, from 1992 to 1995, when I was a mole for the FBI in the largest price fixing scandal in U.S. history. I was an informant with the distinction of being the highest-level Fortune 500 executive ever to be a whistleblower.

The reason I turned against ADM is because of my wife, Ginger. In 1992, Ginger noticed big changes in me. I was involved with price fixing for the past seven months; something the company was involved with over a decade before I even joined ADM. And my work consumed me. She could sense that I was not happy. I was greedy. No matter how much I earned, it was never enough. Although I was not there for Ginger, she had a strength to draw on – her faith. She had a personal relationship with Christ that has sustained her since she was thirteen. In contrast, I went to church, but I was just going through the motions. If someone had asked me in 1992 if I was a Christian I would have said, "Yes, I go to church almost every Sunday."

When Ginger discovered what I was doing, she said I should turn myself into the FBI. I told her I could go to prison and that we would lose our home, our cars and our lifestyle. She retorted that she would rather be homeless than live in a home paid for by theft. She persisted, "Either turn yourself into the FBI, or I will do it for you." And she meant it!

An hour later I was confessing to an FBI agent about my white-collar crime, but it was Ginger who was the true whistleblower of the ADM case. If it was not for a 34-year old stay-at-home mom of three young children, the largest price fixing scheme in U.S. history may never have been exposed.

What would you have done in this situation?

Would you have taken the path I was planning to take: look the other way and continue to move up the corporate ladder with all the perks and financial security? Or would have you taken the path that my wife demanded: confess my part in a serious crime and lose everything?

Ginger understood what it means to be "in the world" and yet not "of the world." She was an "in the world" Christian. I was "of the world" and just trying to look like one.

I confessed and served ten years in prison. There I met Jesus who saved me from my "of the world" living. Today I tell my story all over the country, seeking to help business professionals be Christians, and not just look like one; to be in the world but not of it.

You have finished this incredible book by Dr. Joey and Mike. You now know what I wish I had known before I went to work at ADM. The five core practices of a Faith Positive lifestyle—perceive, conceive, believe, achieve, and receive—truly do increase your faith with greater joy at work so you love God and others more. That's in the world living!

I realize this kind of Faith Positive living is a risk. Just like I faced a decision about which path to take, so do you now.

Will you take the path of working the way you did before you read this book? Will you just look like a Christian, doing business the world's way like I did?

Or, will you choose a different path? The path that takes you through the work world and yet not of it? The path that increases your faith and the faith of those with whom you work and the people you serve? The path that brings you greater joy at work? The path that overflows your heart with love for God and others?

What will you do?

Dr. Joey and Mike have shown you the path in enough detail and simplicity for you to succeed. They have coaching programs to keep you on the path. Take advantage of all of it.

I was living the best life this world has to offer, and I now know that it was not life. My and Ginger's prayer for you is that you choose the path of a Faith Positive life, the one God has destined for you through Jesus Christ, which brings you success here in this world and the next.

Dr. Joey Faucette

is a #1 Amazon best-selling author and ordained minister who has written for Wall Street Journal Market Watch, CNBC, Entrepreneur.com, and countless other websites. He speaks to and coaches business professionals, and serves as an adjunct professor for colleges and divinity schools.

Mike Van Vranken

worked as an insurance agent and executive with a Fortune 50 company for 35 years. He now teaches and speaks to positively influence clergy and laity, writes a monthly column for the Catholic Connection and serves as adjunct professor with the Catholic Diocese of Shreveport.

Go Deeper with the 7 Weeks to Faith Positive Coaching Program

This 7-week video coaching series with downloadable, 24/7-access tools gives you take-action wisdom on the five core practices of a Faith Positive lifestyle so you achieve your spiritual dreams at work including…

- profound yet simple, Scriptural strategies to get unstuck and increase your faith.
- proven, biblical formulas that coach you to move forward with even greater joy at work.
- practical, how-to ways to replace your frustration over work relationships with higher love for God and your customers and teammates.

You receive:

- 7 videos in 7 weeks with 24/7 access for you to grow at your leisure and get a fast-start jump on your Faith Positive lifestyle success.
- Mp3 downloads of the videos so that you learn and listen while driving or working out.
- All the downloadable tools and guides you need to create a more consistent Faith Positive lifestyle today.

Sign up now at GetPositive.Today

Celebrate and Study with
Faith Positive Master Coaching

Increase your faith with greater joy at work so you love God and others more every day. Choose the 24/7 digital access Faith Positive Master Coaching Program package that benefits you best:

Good
- A weekly video for individual study that applies biblical principles to business
- Downloadable guides for customized study
- Mp3 audio of the video for learning on-the-go
- Participation in a Faith Positive Small Group

Better
- "Good" package plus:
- Book-of-the-Month Club: A Kindle book on faith and Christian business practices delivered to your Kindle account.
- Book-of-the-Month Club Author Interview: a 1-hour podcast interview with the author of that month's book.

Best
- "Better" package plus:
- A monthly 1-hour, one-to-one Faith Positive Coaching session with a Faith Positive-certified coach by phone with email support.

Sign up now at GetPositive.Today

Dr. Joey Faucette

Mike Van Vranken

Welcome Faith Positive Partners!

Dr. Joey and Mike welcome Faith Positive Partners—those companies and corporations, churches and denominational groups who wish to resource their employees and members to develop Faith Positive lifestyles.

Partners are regional and/or national judicatories and church groups who wish to equip and encourage ministry with Christian business professionals in their local communities. Partners promote Faith Positive resources to their churches who become Faith Positive Churches for a discounted, one-time investment which purchases an unlimited license for "7 Weeks to Faith Positive" (online or DVD delivery), 20 copies of *Faith Positive in a Negative World* (Kindle or paper), and a one-hour, start-up consultation for the Faith Positive Leader (prefer laity) including leader materials.

Faith Positive Partners are also those companies and corporations who value the spiritual growth of their employees. They become Faith Positive Partners in the same manner as church-related groups. They offer resources to employees directly or through chaplaincy programs.

Sign up now at GetPositive.Today or call 1.877.4DRJOEY and ask for Mike

Made in the USA
Lexington, KY
21 November 2014